Alpha and Omega
52 Weekly Devotionals
Volume II

by

Robert Turnage

ISBN:9798334461437

School of Christ International
P. O. Box 5470 – Beaumont, TX 77726 USA
(409)504-6601
www.schoolofchrist.org
Facebook: School of Christ International

Table of Contents

Foreword	7-8
Week #1 – BRAGGING ON JESUS	9-10
Week #2 – WHEN DOES GOD ANSWER PRAYER	11-12
Week #3 – I KNOW THAT I DO NOT KNOW	13-14
Week #4 – THE LORD OF THE HARVEST	15-16
Week #5 – DOES HELL KNOW YOUR NAME	17-19
Week #6 – JONAH: THE REST OF THE STORY	20-21
Week #7 – IT IS TIME TO STAND UP	22-24
Week #8 – JOY	25-27
Week #9 – DRIVE FORWARD AND SLACK NOT	28-29
Week #10 – YOU HAVE NEVER PASSED THIS WAY BEFORE	30-31
Week #11 – HEAR THE WORD OF THE LORD	32-33
Week #12 – SOMETHING BIGGER THAN YOURSELF	34-35
Week #13 – LORD, IS IT I?	36-37
Week #14 – JESUS IS AUSTERE	38-40
Week #15 – JESUS IS OMNISCIENT	41-42
Week #16 – THE KNOWLEDGE OF THE LORD WILL COVER THE EARTH	43-44
Week #17 – THE GLORY OF THE LORD	45-46
Week #18 – THE ANSWER TO CURRENT WORLD EVENTS	47-48
Week #19 – WHEN GOD IS REJECTED	49-50
Week #20 – PEACE, SAFETY, AND DESTRUCTION	51-52

Week #21 – GUILT BY ASSOCIATION	53-54
Week #22 – SOWING SEEDS IN THE TIME OF FLOOD	55-56
Week #23 – A MOST IMPORTANT DECISION	57-59
Week #24 – MY PRAYER FOR YOU	60-61
Week #25 – MERCY: NOT GETTING THE PUNISHMENT WE DESERVE	62-63
Week #26 – SORROW AND GRIEF	64-65
Week #27 – THE BLESSED	66-67
Week #28 – THE ANTICHRIST	68-69
Week #29 – FAITH	70-71
Week #30 – WHY ME?	72-73
Week #31 – TRIFLING INCIDENTS HAVE BIG EFFECT	74-75
Week #32 – COMPROMISE	76-77
Week #33 – THE NAME ABOVE ALL NAMES	78-79
Week #34 – FUTURE WORLD	80-82
Week #35 – DEFINING THE FINAL JUDGMENT	83-84
Week #36 – PRAY FOR ME	85-86
Week #37 – A GROANING CREATION	87-88
Week #38 – THE BITE OF A SNAKE	89-90
Week #39 – SPIRITUAL EROSION	91-92
Week #40 – THE ALL-INCLUSIVE WORK OF CALVARY	93-94
Week #41 – LOOKING FOR THE 3%	95-96
Week #42 – THAT'S MY KING	97-100
Week #43 – EVERYONE MUST STRIVE TO ENTER HEAVEN	101-102

Week #44 – A TIME TO RISE AND SHINE   103-104

Week #45 – THE SHEPHERD AND THE SHEEP   105-106

Week #46 – TRUTH   107-108

Week #47 – THANKS BE TO GOD   109-110

Week #48 – WHO SHALL I SAY SENT ME?   111-112

Week #49 – MORE VALUABLE THAN GREAT RICHES   113-114

Week #50 – IN ALL THINGS AND FOR ALL THINGS 115-116

Week #51 – GOD'S WORD WILL ALWAYS
        BE PREACHED   117-118

Week #52 – IT WON'T BE LONG (TILL WE'LL BE
        LEAVING HERE)   119-120

FOREWORD

When compiling the Alpha and Omega weekly blog posts for Volume II, it was decided that the first A&O should be the foreword. This message, simply entitled "Alpha and Omega," was written and published by Robert Turnage on April 4th, 2019.

Alpha and Omega

Jesus said in Revelation 1:18, "I am he that liveth, and was dead; and, behold, I am alive for evermore, Amen; and have the keys of hell and of death." As Alpha and Omega, and being alive for evermore, there is nothing or no one else but Christ.

No matter how extensive or complicated a matter everything is complete in Him. Alpha and Omega are the first and last letters in the Greek alphabet. Since there is nothing before or after the beginning and ending everything is compacted and complete in between those two letters. All speech and communication are within the "A" and "Z". Nothing exists outside of that, and nothing goes beyond that.

Colossians 2:9 says, "For in him dwelleth all the fulness of the Godhead bodily." God has made His Son the center and circumference of everything that is, has been or ever will be. Colossians 1:16 says, "For by him were all things created, that are in heaven, and that are in earth, visible and invisible, whether they be thrones, or dominions, or principalities, or powers: all things were created by him, and for him: And he is before all things, and by him all things consist." Further Romans 11:36 says, "For of him, and through him, and to him, are all things: to whom be glory for ever. Amen." That is the sum and total of everything. It is finished and fixed. In Christ any attempt to add or subtract from His Being or purpose will have no effect.

He, as Creator, and as the Supplier of every necessity of man in this world and the world to come, is the only way to redemption. Proverbs 14:12 says, "There is a way which seemeth right unto a man, but the end thereof are the ways of death." Christ as the beginning and the ending declared in Acts 4:12, "Neither is there salvation in any other: for there is none other name under heaven given among men, whereby we must be saved."

Robert Turnage

Robert Turnage
(1943-2022)

Week #1

BRAGGING ON JESUS

Mark 5:19, *"Howbeit Jesus suffered him not, but saith unto him, Go home to thy friends, and tell them how great things the Lord hath done for thee, and hath had compassion on thee."*

I have many great and dear friends who are ministers of the Gospel. The two ministers I am speaking of are brothers. The older brother is deceased, and the remaining brother is advanced in years. The younger brother told me that when he started his preaching ministry, he was scheduled in a church for his first revival. His older brother had been a very successful evangelist for years and concerted to help his brother prepare his sermons for a week of revival services. The younger brother prayed, studied, and was well prepared for each service. He had one week of messages. At the end of the week of revival, the Pastor asked the young preacher to continue for the second week of services. Not having more sermons to preach, he called his brother for advice. The advice given to him was "just get up and brag on Jesus." They had another blessed week of church services.

Many people desire to be an effective witness for Christ but are either intimidated or are bashful. Jesus gave everyone the commission to be a witness, not just by showing a good testimony but also by speaking of the Lord to others. It's not always as complicated as we make it; it is just to brag on Jesus to everyone.

In our scripture from the Gospel of Mark, Jesus said, "...Go home to thy friends, and tell..." We may say I do not know what to say when I witness for Christ. The verse continues, "...tell them how great things the Lord hath done for thee, and hath compassion on thee." That is a great witness and testimony, and actually, all anyone is doing is "bragging on Jesus."

Tell your friends, your mothers, your fathers, your brother and sisters, husbands and wives, and children what God has done for you. Tell of being cleansed by the Blood of Jesus from sin, maybe even from an evil possession. Brag on Jesus for His manifold blessings in health and soundness of mind and financial supply. Tell how He has given you love, joy, and peace. Brag on the finished work of Christ, who has prepared for you a place in Heaven with promise of forever being in His Holy and Righteous presence. Not only is He holy, but John said in his first epistle, *"Beloved, now are we the sons of God, and it doth not yet appear what we shall be: but we know that, when he shall appear, we shall be like him; for we shall see him as he is."* (1 John 3:2)

Of course, all of our boasting and bragging is not about ourselves, but about the transformation change in us by the love of God. Brag on Jesus to everyone you know and meet, telling about what He has done for you.

Week #2

WHEN DOES GOD ANSWER PRAYER?

There is more than one kind of form and reason for people to pray. One form of prayer is a petition to God for an answer that is otherwise impossible. Of course, when an individual prays, they desire an answer, especially when they can do nothing to solve their personal request within themselves. It is recorded in Matthew 19:26, *"But Jesus beheld them, and said unto them, With men this is impossible; but with God all things are possible."* We sometimes question why God does not answer immediately. A significant time between our prayer and God's answer will show us our lack of faith.

The question is, do we really believe God is with us and never leaves us? We have His promise in Matthew 28:20 *"...and, lo, I am with you alway, even unto the end of the world. Amen."*

One gifted author said of this Truth, "All hangs upon this one thing (as simple as it may seem) that if Christ is present (which means nothing else than that God is present), anything is possible at any moment. Are you waiting for someday when things will be better? It is not a matter of time at all; it is a matter of Him. He says, *"I am time and eternity all in a moment, and you need not accept anything in a matter of time; you accept Me, and you may be well-nigh dead in the morning and be very much alive before the day is over."*

Faith will assure the person of prayer that God is not limited by any situation. When we stand in faith, we must know we are not dealing with troubles such as what we can see or that are even a matter of time; we are dealing with the Omniscient, Omnipresent God. Easton's Bible Dictionary defines God's Sovereignty as His "absolute right to do all things according to His own good pleasure." In other words, He is not answerable to a higher power or authority. Therefore, when a believing individual calls upon Him, all Eternity, Power, and Supply are instantly present to answer his prayer.

Anything and everything are immediately possible when He is present. The true and profound Truth concerning prayer is, do we touch God when we pray?

An example is in the story of the death of Lazarus. It's recorded in John 11:39, *"Jesus said, Take ye away the stone. Martha, the sister of him that was dead, saith unto him, Lord, by this time he stinketh: for he hath been dead four days."* That's an impossible situation for any man. But Jesus, not waiting on any particular situation or particular timing, the Bible says, *"...when he thus had spoken, he cried with a loud voice, Lazarus, come forth. And he that was dead came forth..." (John 11:43-44).*

Take everything to God in prayer remembering His Promise in 1 John 5:14-15, *"And this is the confidence that we have in him, that, if we ask any thing according to his will, he heareth us: And if we know that he hear us, whatsoever we ask, we know that we have the petitions that we desired of him."*

Week #3

I KNOW THAT I DO NOT KNOW

God said in Isaiah 55:8-9, *"For my thoughts are not your thoughts, neither are your ways my ways, saith the Lord. For as the heavens are higher than the earth, so are my ways higher than your ways, and my thoughts than your thoughts."*

In a time when great emphasis is placed on learning and intellect, sometimes the greatest admission is "I do not know." I'm certainly not making an appeal for ignorance but making the point that man's increase in knowledge is not as great and clear as he thinks it is. The fact is until a person is educated and learned in the things of God; he is not fully educated. No one will ever know all of the things and ways of God, even in eternity. Throughout all eternity, the glorified saint will be learning eternal truths of the Almighty.

None can know the wisdom of God. In the book of Job, God reveals His sole authorship in creation. The Almighty's first question to Job was, *"Where wast thou when I laid the foundation of the earth?..."* (Job 38:4) Through the remainder of that chapter, God schools Job on every aspect of the creation. The Apostle Paul adds in Colossians 1:16-17, *"For by him were all things created, that are in heaven, and that are in earth, visible and invisible, whether they be thrones, or dominions, or principalities, or powers: all things were created by him, and for him: And he is before all things, and by him all things consist."* Paul further says of the wisdom and knowledge of God in Romans 11:33-36, *"O the depth of the riches both of the wisdom and knowledge of God! how unsearchable are his judgments, and his ways past finding out! For who hath known the mind of the Lord?*

or who hath been his counsellor? Or who hath first given to him, and it shall be recompensed unto him again? For of him, and through him, and to him, are all things:to whom be glory forever. Amen."

If I can't find Him out, know how and why such marvelous and unspeakable things are done by and through Him. So, what then is man to do in serving a God with such truths concerning Him? This question is directly answered in Ecclesiastes 12:13 *"Let us hear the conclusion of the whole matter: Fear God, and keep his commandments: for this is the whole duty of man."*

The Bible gives us His revealed Person to us. I know that I do not know. I know He is the only Savior. By faith, I know that salvation is by the redemptive Blood of Jesus, but I do not know how He does it. By faith, I know that He is the baptizer in the Holy Ghost, but I do not know how He does that. By faith, I know He is the Healer, but I do not know how He accomplishes that. By faith, I know He will return to gather all His children, but I do not know how that will be fulfilled.

Until God finishes His work and purpose for us here on earth, and we have understanding, we will rejoice knowing, *"And God shall wipe away all tears from their eyes; and there shall be no more death, neither sorrow, nor crying, neither shall there be any more pain: for the former things are passed away"* (Revelation 21:4).

Week #4

THE LORD OF THE HARVEST

In the earlier years of my ministry, I was approached late at night by a car full of angry young men that said they were going to kill me. The testimony is too long to tell in this setting, and I thank God for keeping me safe. I was preaching a revival, and one night a young man attended a service of the revival. To make a long story short, he was saved by the grace of God, and after a considerable length of time, he married the daughter of the Pastor where I was holding the revival. Over a period of time, I was able to put the story of my experience together. The young man that was saved had been a gang member. He once told me, "The boys that came to kill you that night were members of the gang I was a part of. When they learned I had been saved, though they knew nothing about the forgiveness of sins, they thought that I would confess my gang experience to you, and they felt they could not let that happen." (He never told me anything except he could clear up some matters that had taken place in a larger city close to where they lived.) He told me his former friends would have definitely killed me.

There is only one unpardonable sin, and that is to sin against the Spirit of God. God loves a sinner and will forgive him of all manner of sin, even murder. Though I knew nothing of this story when he first entered our service, God showed His great love for a young man, and through repentance and surrender to God, he was saved. I thank God I preached the message, and with others prayed him through to the new birth that changed his eternal destiny from Hell to Heaven. I have always thought that was the purpose of the ministry. Jesus said of Himself in doing the will of the Father, *"For the Son of man is come to seek and to save that which was lost."* (Luke 19:10)

In Matthew 9:38, Jesus said, *"Pray ye therefore the Lord of the harvest, that he will send forth labourers into his harvest."* The Apostle Peter, speaking by the Holy Spirit, said in 1 Peter 2:21, *"For even hereunto were ye called: because Christ also suffered for us, leaving us an example, that ye should follow his steps..."* The example Jesus left us includes how He went through all the towns and villages, teaching in their synagogues, proclaiming the good news of the kingdom, and healing every disease and sickness. Jesus was *"...despised and rejected of men..."* (Isaiah 53:3). But remember His words in John 15:18, *"If the world hate you, ye know that it hated me before it hated you."*

Many times, we do not feel we are capable of standing in the face of serious and imminent danger, but God is with us and keeps us through every experience. As a part of the above story, I later went through a period of fear. I make no claim to be bold or sufficient for that kind of test, but at that moment when I thought of what could have happened, God spoke His precious words from Matthew 10:28, *"And fear not them which kill the body, but are not able to kill the soul: but rather fear him which is able to destroy both soul and body in hell."* May we all be strong in the Lord and follow in His steps.

Week #5

DOES HELL KNOW YOUR NAME?

"And the evil spirit answered and said, Jesus I know, and Paul I know; but who are ye?" Acts 19:15

Some people say they desire to see God do great things in this generation, even equal to His works in the Bible. Since Jesus is always the same (Hebrews 13:8) and assured us, it is His good pleasure and will to bless us and meet our every need (Philippians 2:13), why do we not have what we say we are longing for? One reason, and there are many, is we drawback when the devil fights against us. But there is, and there always will be, a time for the Christian to resist and stand firm against the adversary. The enemy is not going to let us receive from God without a severe and significant battle. I believe when God meets and supplies our needs, the devil hates us even more than ever. He hates the blessing we receive because, before he was cast out, he received the blessings of God which we now receive and enjoy. The devil is the destroyer, and since he lost his place in heaven, it is his goal to keep everyone from receiving from God.

In our text, the evil spirit, an imp of hell and worker of the devil said, *"...Jesus I know."* By and through the death, burial, and resurrection of Christ, he knows his final destruction and destination. Revelation 20:10 gives this record, *"And the devil that deceived them was cast into the lake of fire and brimstone, where the beast and the false prophet are, and shall be tormented day and night for ever and ever."*

God anointed the Apostle Paul, and he, through God, defeated and withstood the devil. In the book of Acts, it says, *"And God wrought special miracles by the hands of Paul: So that from his body were brought unto the sick handkerchiefs or aprons, and the diseases departed from them, and the evil spirits went out of them."* (Acts 19:11-12) Yes, the evil spirit and hell knew Paul. In Acts 16:17, is one record of how he was instrumental in leading sinners from the ruin of hell to the love of God. It reads, *"The same followed Paul and us, and cried, saying, These men are the servants of the most high God, which shew unto us the way of salvation."* Paul spoke to Agrippa of Christ in Acts 26:28, *"Then Agrippa said unto Paul, almost thou persuadest me to be a Christian."*

From being a persecutor of the people of Christ to eventually making four missionary journeys, he declared to all peoples, *"But I say, Have they not heard? Yes verily, their sound went into all the earth, and their words unto the ends of the world."* (Romans 10:18)

Yes, everything evil and devilish knows the name of an overcomer who has not withdrawn from the violent and vicious battles against the kingdom of darkness and its devil, demons, evil and unclean spirits.

In 2nd Corinthians eleven, verses 24-27, the Apostle provides a partial list of his experiences in the Gospel for Christ. He said in part, *"Of the Jews five times received I forty stripes save one. Thrice was I beaten with rods, once was I stoned, thrice I suffered shipwreck, a night and a day I have been in the deep; In journeyings often, in perils of waters, in perils of robbers, in perils by mine own countrymen, in perils by the heathen, in perils in the city, in perils in the wilderness, in perils in the sea, in perils among false brethren; In weariness and painfulness, in watchings often, in hunger and thirst, in fastings often, in cold and nakedness."*

Yet he also had these testimonies. In Philippians 4:13, he rightly declared *"I can do all things through Christ which strengtheneth me."* Then he said in Acts 20:24, *"But none of these things move me, neither count I my life dear unto myself, so that I might finish my course with joy, and the ministry, which I have received of the Lord Jesus, to testify the gospel of the grace of God."* Another testimony of this man is found in 2 Timothy 4:8, *"Henceforth there is laid up for me a crown of righteousness, which the Lord, the righteous judge, shall give me at that day: and not to me only, but unto all them also that love his appearing."*

It's time for hell to know again the names of God's holy people operating by the power of His Spirit and Name. God has and will have a people known and feared by hell because of the works of Him in their lives.

Week #6

JONAH: THE REST OF THE STORY

We are all familiar with the story of Jonah, or are we?

We rejoice at the five thousand and the three thousand that were saved in the New Testament by the preaching of the disciples and apostles. But less mention is given to this Old Testament story about the city of Nineveh. In that city, 120,000 were saved. In the New Testament, the believers and followers of Jesus rejoiced at the work that was done. They were overjoyed and testified to this miracle. None of them were mad at God for delivering these people out of the darkness and leading them into the Light. They had a desire to preach and lead multitudes of others to the Lord continually. They labored, were lied on, were beaten by unbelievers, only to go from city to city to bear witness to the Savior. They loved not their lives unto death but counted it all joy, in the face of all opposition, to preach Jesus Christ and Him crucified.

All of God's people have a responsibility to the unsaved. Not just the preacher or missionary. We are all living witnesses for Christ; we are to make disciples (disciplined ones) of the unsaved. Indeed, how can they be saved without a preacher (messenger) to speak to them?

Now take a look at the record of Jonah; he gets a Divine call from God. Jonah 1:1-2, *"Now the word of the LORD came unto Jonah the son of Amittai, saying, Arise, go to Nineveh, that great city, and cry against it; for their wickedness is come up before me."* Following Jonah's experience in the storm and the belly of the fish, the Lord reappeared to Jonah and commanded in Jonah 3:1-2,

"And the word of the LORD came unto Jonah the second time, saying, Arise, go unto Nineveh, that great city, and preach unto it the preaching that I bid thee." In chapter 3, there is fasting and repentance, and instead of judgment coming in forty days, they have been accepted of God (Jonah 3:5-10). One would think Jonah would be as excited at 120,000 being converted as the messengers were when 5,000 and 3,000 were converted in Jerusalem. But look at what is recorded in Jonah 4:1-3, *"But it displeased Jonah exceedingly, and he was very angry. And he prayed unto the LORD, and said, I pray thee, O LORD, was not this my saying when I was yet in my country? Therefore I fled before unto Tarshish: for I knew that thou art a gracious God, and merciful, slow to anger, and of great kindness, and repentest thee of the evil. Therefore now, O LORD, take, I beseech thee, my life from me; for it is better for me to die than to live."* An entire city is saved, and the inerrant Word of God said, *"But it displeased Jonah exceedingly, and he was very angry..."*

A person may not be entirely wrong to say Jonah was selfish, and he had no eternal interest in Nineveh. It may be possible that if he had his way, the entire city could have gone to hell.

In the end, though Jonah had his way for a time, God humbled him and had His way in Jonah's life. God wanted Nineveh saved and showed them His love, mercy, and forgiveness through a man such as Jonah.

Week #7

IT IS TIME TO STAND UP

In the book of Esther, when Mordecai encouraged Esther to go before King Ahasuerus, the king could have sent her to her death. All Mordecai knew was that SOMETHING HAD TO BE DONE IMMEDIATELY! So rather than do nothing, he began to take action against the condition where he was. Esther had not been summoned before King Ahasuerus for thirty days, and a person could be put to death for going uninvited before the king. If the king did not extend his scepter, she would have been killed. She knew that, but knowing what was at stake, she willfully put herself in that place of risk. *"...if I perish, I perish."* (Esther 4:16)

There is not much information regarding Mordecai in the book of Esther, except he was of the tribe of Benjamin. When he heard of an evil plan against the people of God, he undoubtedly knew he had to do something against their enemy. No matter who he was or what his future plans were, he stepped up and put his life on the line also. He involved himself in a Holy battle against anyone and everyone who stood against the people of God. When Esther's father and mother died, Mordecai being a relative of her father, raised Esther as his own daughter. He would never have put her in danger of death, but given the plans of the enemy, he knew nothing or no one was expendable. The fact is certain death is the story of this book. Someone or some people will die. The death sentence was not only on Esther but every Jew in the empire of King Ahasuerus. It was a time of life and death.

The Name of God is not mentioned one time in the book of Esther, but He is there, and He is working to bring deliverance and victory to those facing death. An example of His working is that Mordecai learns of a plot to assassinate the king. He sends word to the king, and not only is the plot averted, but on a sleepless night, the king reads in the chronicles of Mordecai's role in saving his life. Haman who was a government minister of the king and who despised Mordecai had to lead Mordecai dressed in King Ahasuerus' apparel and jewelry and riding the king's horse through the streets to the acclaim of the people.

This story has a great ending. Haman is hanged on a gallows he had built to hang Mordecai on, the Jews are spared execution and peace abounds. That is the only way God works. Don't be afraid, go before even a possible death sentence, stand against wicked and corrupt leaders, turn everything over to God and rejoice in His ways. That is the result and the end of the story.

What goes before this outcome is the testimony of people who risked their lives. They were willing to die for who and what they believed in and went to work. That was the testimony of Queen Esther and Mordecai.

God has a plan and will for our generation. Will it be said of us, as it was of David in Acts 13:36, *"...for David, after he had served his own generation by the will of God..."* or will we be ashamed before God for abandoning this generation. We are facing the last days, and lives are in the balance. Where are this generation's Esther and Mordecai? Are we going to be indifferent to God's will for us and our stance for Him or just hope someone else will stand in that place? As for me and my house, we want to stand in the power of His Might. We want to hear Him say we have done well. The battle is now before us. The hour of need is now. We must individually make up our minds. Are we fully prepared to answer Paul's urging in Romans 12:1 when he said,

"I beseech you therefore, brethren, by the mercies of God, that ye present your bodies a living sacrifice, holy, acceptable unto God, which is your reasonable service." Without going into personal feelings etc. I know for me this is a major stand, based on the fact I am no hero, and I do not make brash statements. I am trusting God will supply all needed grace in all times of need.

I heard Pastor Clendennen say on one occasion that: "THE GREATEST CONCERN IS THERE IS NO CONCERN!"

As with Esther, we have undoubtedly *"...come to the kingdom for such a time as this."* (Esther 4:14)

Week #8

JOY

In speaking of Christ in Hebrews 12:2, it says, *"Looking unto Jesus the author and finisher of our faith; who for the joy that was set before him endured the cross, despising the shame, and is set down at the right hand of the throne of God."* It speaks of Christ's suffering on the cross, His endurance, and His accompanying shame before He had rest. What is equally noteworthy to His death and suffering is how He lived with the pain and why He did so. In all of His dying and death experience, it was all served in joy—what an incredible testimony. The death of Christ on the cross was indescribable, for His death was one in which the Innocent died for the guilty. To be hanged on a cross was a curse for any man. Galatians 3:13 speaks of this death, saying, *"Christ hath redeemed us from the curse of the law, being made a curse for us: for it is written, Cursed is every one that hangeth on a tree."* The prophet Isaiah, speaking of the death of Jesus, indicates that He was not recognizable as a man when He described Him with these words, *"As many were astonied at thee; his visage was so marred more than any man, and his form more than the sons of men"* (Isaiah 52:14). Remember the writing in Hebrews 12:2, *"...who for the joy that set before Him..."*

The King James Version Dictionary defines joy as "the passion or emotion excited by the acquisition or expectation of good; that excitement of pleasurable feelings which is caused by success, good fortune, the gratification of desire or some good possessed, or by a rational prospect of possessing what we love or desire; gladness; exultation; the exhilaration of spirits. Joy is a delight of the mind, from the consideration of the present or assured approaching possession of a good. Bring heavenly balm to heal my country's wounds, Joy to my soul, and transport to my lay."

Those who seek this world's definition of joy, through sin and carnality, do not know true joy. Paul said in 1 Timothy 5:6, *"But she that liveth in pleasure is dead while she liveth."* Many are dead while they are still live. Romans 14:17 defines and tells the source of real joy, *"For the kingdom of God is not meat and drink; but righteousness, and peace, and joy in the Holy Ghost."* Anyone, no matter their sufferings and hardships in this life, can live every moment in joy when you live in the kingdom of God and see the real purpose of life just as Jesus did in Hebrews 12:2. We are and will be faced with many tribulations, as can be seen in Psalms 34:19, *"Many are the afflictions of the righteous…"* but accompanied with the Lord's assurance *"…but the LORD delivereth him out of them all."* Moses had a comparable experience and came out the victor as seen in Hebrews 11:24-26, *"By faith Moses, when he was come to years, refused to be called the son of Pharaoh's daughter; Choosing rather to suffer affliction with the people of God, than to enjoy the pleasures of sin for a season; Esteeming the reproach of Christ greater riches than the treasures in Egypt: for he had respect unto the recompense of the reward."*

For the child of God, their joy is found in living totally for Christ, no matter what the sufferings for a season may be, doing the Will of the Father, and giving their all for sinners that need Christ. Jesus said of Himself when preparing to die for lost souls and facing the agony of the cross *"…Father, save me from this hour: but for this cause came I unto this hour"* (John 12:27). He issues us His desire that we would pray until the sinner *"And that they may recover themselves out of the snare of the devil, who are taken captive by him at his will"* (2 Timothy

2:26). I sincerely pray that you will receive and live in the true joy of the Lord.

Week #9

DRIVE FORWARD AND SLACK NOT

"Then she saddled an ass, and said to her servant, Drive, and go forward; slack not thy riding for me, except I bid thee" (2 Kings 4:24). These are the words of a desperate lady to her servant. She and her husband had shown great kindness to the prophet Elisha for a long time by supplying him food and rest during his ministry. The Bible refers to her as a *"great"* woman *(2 Kings 4:8)* and that she recognized Elisha to be *"...an holy man of God..." (2 Kings 4:9)*. This lady and her husband eventually built a chamber with a bed and some furnishings for Elisha to occupy when he would journey through that area. The prophet was appreciative and desired to show kindness for all that had been done for him. The prophet and his servant questioned this lady about what they could do for her. She did not have an answer. Elisha's servant, Gehazi, told the man of God the woman had no children. The prophet told this childless barren lady, with an old husband, that according to the time of life, she was going to conceive and bare a son. She asked the prophet not to lie to her. But as Elisha had promised her a child, she bares a son.

In the continuance of time, this miracle son went to his father, who was working with the reapers. The boy complained to his father that his head was hurting. The father instructed a lad to take him to his mother. He sat on his mother's knee until noon and died *(2 Kings 4:20)*. The mother needed another miracle, and she knew how to receive one. She laid her miracle son now dead on the bed that was the same as placing him on an altar of prayer before God. She called for and was placed on an ass with a servant to goad him and direct the ass to find the prophet of God. She knew there was another mighty work of God to be done for her. This is the situation surrounding the text, *"Then she saddled an ass, and said to her servant, Drive, and go forward; slack not thy riding for me, except I bid thee" (2 Kings 4:24).* She has another impossible (with man) crisis. She is not going to allow anything or anyone to get in the way of getting to the place where she can take her son home again. To the servant, she was saying keep going, make haste, and don't slow the pace. I have been given the desire of my heart, a gift from God, and death has taken him from me. This journey took between six and eight hours, but her directive was clear. She was saying you don't pay any attention to my advanced age, weariness, or anything else. Just get me to the man of God. When Elisha prayed the boy was raised from the dead and returned to his mother *(2 Kings 4:36).*

This is a true and exciting story to read. It will encourage your heart, place within you a determination to get to God for the answer to your prayer. One of the devils devices against a child of God, is discouragement. Be strong in the Lord, and He will fulfill His promises.

Week #10

YOU HAVE NEVER PASSED THIS WAY BEFORE

When Joshua led the people of God to where they would soon cross the Jordan River, the people lodged by the river for three days. After three days the officers went through the host of the people *"And they commanded the people, saying, When ye see the ark of the covenant of the LORD your God, and the priests the Levites bearing it, then ye shall remove from your place, and go after it. Yet there shall be a space between you and it, about two thousand cubits by measure: come not near unto it, that ye may know the way by which ye must go: for ye have not passed this way heretofore. "* (Joshua 3:3-4).

There is much more to this long-ago testimony of the perfect leading of God at that time. It is relative and very crucial to our present time, July 2020. A study of this experience has several truths that are almost hidden to us today. One thing they were facing was a transition. One writer said, "...the Jordan represented a place of transition—in fact, of new beginnings—it became the place where John baptized Jesus. The Jordan was a place of transition that remains an enduring symbol. The transition that occurred there were sometimes national—as with Moses and Joshua, Elijah and Elisha, and John and Jesus."

In their heart, they may have been asking, "what is going on"? After all the times of tremendous troubles these people had gone through, they could be worried and anxious about the coming days and time.

They were told what they were to do in verse 3 *"...When ye see the ark of the covenant of the LORD your God, and the priests the Levites bearing it, then ye shall remove from your place, and go after it."* God, who was leading them, said they were to follow the ark and those who God had instructed to lead them. When I said there was a lesson for us today in times of wondering about the direction of events, He still says when there is a time of transition, just follow Me. These people followed God, and He told them all they needed to know. What they had to do was obey. When God is leading His own people, everything becomes clear. Everyone must obey and follow His Divine leadership.

Again, in verse 4, they were not only instructed what to do but why they were to do them. The instructions on this journey of transition were *"...there shall be a space between you and it, about two thousand cubits by measure: come not near unto it, that ye may know the way by which ye must go: for ye have not passed this way heretofore."*

An earlier generation of the church sang a song that "the Lord knows the way through the wilderness; all you have to do is follow." Hold on child of God for we are told in Job 23:10, *"But he knoweth the way that I take: when he hath tried me, I shall come forth as gold."*

Week #11

HEAR THE WORD OF THE LORD

The prophet Jeremiah cried out, *"O earth, earth, earth, hear the word of the LORD" (Jeremiah 22:29)*. The three references to the word *"earth"* alerts to profound and extreme dangers, interests, and warnings. To us today, these words would be interpreted to say, "O America, America, America, hear the word of the LORD." We may not fully understand everything He is saying and will yet speak to us, but He will faithfully come to us. In Matthew 11:15, Jesus said, *"He that hath ears to hear, let him hear,"* is for us now. I pray we do not sleep in indifference and unconcern, while the Voice of God is speaking. One ancient commentator suggests, "...one reason of this threefold appellation was because the land of Israel was divided into three parts, Judea, beyond Jordan, and Galilee; hear the word of the Lord; which follows." A well-known and respected commentator, born in 1697, said by repeating the word "earth" three times (was) "...to rebuke the stupidity of the people and to quicken their attention to somewhat very remarkable and worthy of notice..." word of God that would follow. There is enough stupidity in this church generation. God is speaking to His messengers, so they, in turn, may speak the Truth of God to the people.

It is generally believed that the Word of God in Isaiah 6:8, *"Also I heard the voice of the Lord, saying, Whom shall I send, and who will go for us? Then said I, Here am I; send me"* is in reference to missionaries and their works in foreign lands. It certainly includes these ministers, but it is better understood in light of the words of Jesus in Mark 13:37, *"And what I say unto you I say unto all, Watch."* All the Words of Jesus are timeless and always current to every generation. It is crucial that we have the same heart and right spirit of Isaiah and say to God, "Here I am; send me." God is still calling and sending His true messengers.

I do not have the words to say what my heart feels and how deeply I cry out for God to continue to use and increase our place in today's spiritually bankrupt and sick world that so desperately needs God. Please join with all of our brothers and sisters in what is a closing window of opportunity as Jesus prepares to come for His saints and then... (You fill in the blank).

Week #12

SOMETHING BIGGER THAN YOURSELF

Many, many times I heard my pastor, B. H. Clendennen, say that everyone needs something in their life bigger than themselves. When speaking to me of my ministry, he repeated that on several occasions. I heeded that advice and it has been a part of my life and ministry since I received this profound help. He not only preached that but throughout my life's experience with him I observed he loyally practiced his own words.

Sometime in the late '50s or early '60s, before I met him, he had an evangelist at his church. In that revival, the evangelist practiced and preached much on prayer. He called for early morning prayer services during the revival. Many people of the church joined the evangelist and Pastor Clendennen at 5 AM to seek God. The evangelist moved on, and except for a much smaller number of church people, Pastor Clendennen continued to pray at 5 AM until he died in 2009. He not only preached and taught the necessity of prayer but called our church to days and weeks of prayer throughout the year. Every service at our church was always proceeded by at least 30 minutes of prayer. Not only was prayer called but also seasons of fasting. Every October the pastor would fast 30 days, and ask the church people to fast as often as their health, age, etc. would allow. I could include so many more examples of his personal commitment to the Lord and His work. He continued to call all of God's people to have something in their life bigger than themselves. None is bigger than God. Nothing is bigger in our lives than to do His will and work. I am not exalting a man, he would never approve of that, but I am only describing life as it was for him and his leadership to the followers of Christ. I only wish I could and would have observed more faithfully the example, he not only told me about but showed me.

What kind of an example are we living and way of life are we showing to our present generation, and an even younger generation that we are preaching to. Is everything in our life for our convenience, our comfort, and our desires? To reach this world, that is showing evidence of coming to an end with the soon return of Christ, is going to require being totally sold out to Christ, unselfish, Spirit-filled Christian people that believe the desires and will of God is bigger than our personal goals and feelings.

Week #13

LORD, IS IT I?

In Matthew 22, Jesus is eating the Passover meal with His disciples. On this occasion, He tells them the hour of His betrayal, suffering, and crucifixion was at hand. He also said to them that one of them would betray Him, at that point each of His disciples, including Judas, asked, *"...Lord, is it I?"* (Matthew 26:22). Judas referred to Him as Master and asked, *"...Master, is it I?"* (Matthew 26:25). The Lord's response to the disciples' questions was directed to Judas with three words, *"...Thou hast said."*

We are told to examine and prove ourselves in 2 Corinthians 13:5. In 1 Corinthians 11:28, Paul said, *"...let a man examine himself..."* In the book of Lamentations 3:40, the prophet says we must *"...search and try our ways..."*

Many people think too highly of themselves to either be examined or examine themselves. Romans 12:3 encourages us to let *"...every man that is among you, not to think of himself more highly than he ought to think."* In churches, believers are critical of one another when we are told, *"Let nothing be done through strife or vainglory; but in lowliness of mind let each esteem other better than themselves"* (Philippians 2:3). It would prove to be an overcoming victory and would be blessed by God if we would be as the disciples when they questioned Jesus, *"Lord, is it I?"* God himself said in Acts 13:22, *"...I have found David the son of Jesse, a man after mine own heart..."* David wrote in Psalms 119: 59 how he reached the place of God's testimony of him when he said, *"I thought on my ways, and turned my feet unto thy testimonies."*

It seems there is a carnality of life that prevents us from viewing ourselves in the light of Scripture and our obedience to it. There is a Divine conclusion to this matter of judging others and our day in God's courts. Revelation 20:12 says, *"And I saw the dead, small and great, stand before God; and the books were opened: and another book was opened, which is the book of life: and the dead were judged out of those things which were written in the books, according to their works."* I humbly ask of God today, according to Psalms 139:23-24, *"Search me, O God, and know my heart: try me, and know my thoughts: And see if there be any wicked way in me, and lead me in the way everlasting."* I do not say that out of self-righteousness but in an earnest plea before God. God bless you in your walk with God.

Week #14

JESUS IS AUSTERE

When it comes to the mention of money in regard to the Kingdom of God, many, if not most, people can be offended. Jesus actually had a lot to say about the purpose of money and the amount given. Some misquote Scripture to satisfy their attack on giving in obedience to the Word of God and supporting the continuance of the work of God. In Mark 12:41-44 is the story of the widows' mite. Her entire living, which, according to Bible helps amounted to two small copper coins (about a penny). That was the actual worldly monetary value. Jesus stated that her one penny offering was a significantly larger gift than all of the others. *" And Jesus sat over against the treasury, and beheld how the people cast money into the treasury: and many that were rich cast in much. And there came a certain poor widow, and she threw in two mites, which make a farthing. And he called unto him his disciples, and saith unto them, Verily I say unto you, That this poor widow hath cast more in, than all they which have cast into the treasury: For all they did cast in of their abundance; but she of her want did cast in all that she had, even all her living. "* (Mark 12:41-44). Jesus was sitting and observing everyone's giving. He acknowledged the amounts placed in the treasury and spoke to His disciples about the liberality of this *"poor widow"* (Mark 12:21). He knew that everyone else had given out of their abundance, but she of her want did cast in all that she had, even all her living. Jesus knew the amount given by each contributor and what percentage was for Him and His interest versus their personal desires and ambitions.

Jesus observed that which was given to Him in these verses, but in speaking to His disciples on another occasion, He addressed the subject of their almsgiving. The Bible dictionary defines alms as "the act of charity toward those less fortunate." In the Apostolic age, Christians were taught that giving alms was an expression of love which was first expressed by God to them in that Jesus sacrificed Himself as an act of love for the salvation of believers. Jesus spoke with specificity about this in Matthew 6:1-4 when He said, *" Take heed that ye do not your alms before men, to be seen of them: otherwise ye have no reward of your Father which is in heaven. Therefore when thou doest thine alms, do not sound a trumpet before thee, as the hypocrites do in the synagogues and in the streets, that they may have glory of men. Verily I say unto you, They have their reward. But when thou doest alms, let not thy left hand know what thy right hand doeth: That thine alms may be in secret: and thy Father which seeth in secret himself shall reward thee openly. "* It was in almsgiving that Jesus said, *"...let not thy left hand know what thy right hand doeth:"* (Matthew 6:3).

Another reference to Jesus and money is found in the 19th chapter of the book of Luke. In that chapter, Jesus has given talents (money or value) to three individuals that were to be used in His interest. Two of the recipients had invested and increased the amount they received. The third man, who had received the smallest amount to invest, when Jesus questioned him about the enlargement of his money to be used for Christ he said to Jesus, *"For I feared thee, because thou art an austere man: thou takest up that thou layedst not down, and reapest that thou didst not sow."* The man's defense is found in verse 21 *"...because thou art an austere man..."* Jesus never refuted his words. Jesus said to the man in verse 22, *"...Thou knewest that I was an austere man..."* In verse 22, Jesus said, *"...I will judge thee, thou wicked servant..."*

The meaning of austere in the KJV Bible Dictionary is *"severe; harsh; rigid; stern; applied to persons; as an austere master; an austere look."*

Jesus continues to observe the treasury and our obedient response to it. God help us not to grieve our "austere" Christ.

Week #15

GOD IS OMNISCIENT

When writing about our Holy God, by the Holy Spirit, the Prophet Isaiah said in chapter 44 and verse 6, *"Thus saith the LORD the King of Israel, and his redeemer the LORD of hosts; I am the first, and I am the last; and beside me there is no God."* Again, from the book of Isaiah, God said, *"...I am the LORD, and there is none else, there is no God beside me..."* (Isaiah 45:5). Among the attributes of our eternally existent God is Omnipotence, which declares He is "all-powerful." He is also Omnipresence, which is His "presence as being everywhere." The Omniscients of God is He is "all-knowing."

A look at the all-knowing attribute of God, Omniscient we see it comes from two Latin words: "Omnis," which means "all" and "Scientia," which means "knowledge." One writer said, "When Christians say God is omniscient, they mean that God knows all things — the past, present, and future. God is the source of all knowledge, and God also knows all the potentialities of any situation. God knows every person's thoughts — even before they think it." In the Bible Dictionary, the adjective to Omniscient means "knowing everything."

In his life, David, the patriarch, knew the all-knowing reality of God. In Psalms 139:1-4, *"O LORD, thou hast searched me, and known me. Thou knowest my downsitting and mine uprising, thou understandest my thought afar off. Thou compassest my path and my lying down, and art acquainted with all my ways. For there is not a word in my tongue, but, lo, O LORD, thou knowest it altogether."*

In the late 1940s, Christian author A.W. Tozer wrote in the book The Pursuit of God, "He is Omniscient, which means that He knows in one free and effortless act all matter, all spirit, all relationships, all events. Our knowledge is limited, and our best efforts at understanding are finite. Our own experiences trap us in a specific place and time. God's knowledge is unlimited. Knowing that God is Omniscient should cause us to trust His Will, His Word, and His Timing. Though we do not know all the answers, God does."

We must learn to trust in the fact that God knows all concerning us and will not lead us astray. We need to learn to be at peace as long as we follow the Lord and walk faithfully in His ways for us.

Week #16

THE KNOWLEDGE OF THE LORD WILL COVER THE EARTH

Isaiah 14:12-15 gives us the record of Satan being cast out of heaven; *"How art thou fallen from heaven, O Lucifer, son of the morning! how art thou cut down to the ground, which didst weaken the nations! For thou hast said in thine heart, I will ascend into heaven, I will exalt my throne above the stars of God: I will sit also upon the mount of the congregation, in the sides of the north: I will ascend above the heights of the clouds; I will be like the most High. Yet thou shalt be brought down to hell, to the sides of the pit."* In verse 12, he is called *"...Lucifer, son of the morning."* In verse 15, he is given his sentence of eternal punishment *"... thou shalt be brought down to hell, to the sides of the pit."* There is a reason for the actions of God. Lucifer fell because of his sin against God. Proverbs 26:2 says, *"...the curse causeless shall not come."*

Revelation 12:7-10 reveals some of what had transpired in heaven that Satan would be changed from his exalted position to his final punishment in hell. It reads, *"And there was war in heaven: Michael and his angels fought against the dragon; and the dragon fought and his angels, And prevailed not; neither was their place found any more in heaven. And the great dragon was cast out, that old serpent, called the Devil, and Satan, which deceiveth the whole world: he was cast out into the earth, and his angels were cast out with him. And I heard a loud voice saying in heaven, Now is come salvation, and strength, and the kingdom of our God, and the power of his Christ: for the accuser of our brethren is cast down, which accused them before our God day and night."*

The devil is described as a dragon, a liar, a tempter, a deceiver, an adversary, an enemy, a serpent, a thief, and the angel of the abyss, to name a few of his names and titles.

As he made war in heaven and since he was cast out of heaven, he has made war in the earth. He is the enemy of everyone, as revealed in John 10:10, *"The thief cometh not, but for to steal, and to kill, and to destroy..."* his utter defeat and place in the bottomless pit. The book of Revelation, chapter 20, verses 1-3, declares *"And I saw an angel come down from heaven, having the key of the bottomless pit and a great chain in his hand. And he laid hold on the dragon, that old serpent, which is the Devil, and Satan, and bound him a thousand years, And cast him into the bottomless pit, and shut him up, and set a seal upon him, that he should deceive the nations no more..."*

A study of God's sure Word in Habakkuk 2:14 tells of a time when *"For the earth shall be filled with the knowledge of the glory of the LORD, as the waters cover the sea."* The devil came to steal the truth and to rob man of the fullness of God's Word, but this scripture shows the fulfillment of God's eternal plan. This verse does not imply that everyone is going to come to Christ, but that the knowledge of Him will cover the earth as the waters cover the sea.

Week #17

THE GLORY OF GOD

The Bible Dictionary, in reference to the Glory of God, says, "...it is sometimes stated that God's Glory is the external manifestation of His being." After providing references and comments to that belief in the dictionary, they concluded with this statement, "God's Glory exists prior to and apart from any manifestation of it (His Glory)." Indeed, His Glory was with Him in the beginning, and He never changes. In Isaiah 42:8, God said of His Glory, *"I am the LORD: that is my name: and my glory will I not give to another..."* All Glory is His, but Christians are instructed to *"Let your light shine before men, that they may see your good works, and glorify your Father which is in heaven"* (Matthew 5:16). Our good works here are speaking of our witnessing, courage, zeal, faithfulness, and diligence.

A person can expect severe satanic attacks when they are doing God's work, and God is with them and blessing them. John 12:10-11 says of Lazarus, *"But the chief priests consulted that they might put Lazarus also to death; Because that by reason of him many of the Jews went away, and believed on Jesus."* Lazarus' testimony and his following Christ put him in danger of death. For the Glory of God, we could face even death.

But John 14:13 tells us that all things are done *"...that the Father may be glorified in the Son."* Everything in our life and experience should be for the Glory of God. That is the reason His people are experiencing many of the sorrows and sufferings they are presently experiencing in this life. In John chapter 9, Jesus answered the questions of the people regarding the sickness of a man, and for whose sins had caused it. Jesus said, *"Neither hath this man sinned, nor his parents: but that the works of God should be made manifest in him"* (John 9:3). Everything is for the Glory of God.

In Exodus 33:18-19, Moses said to the Lord, *"...I beseech thee, shew me thy glory. And he said, I will make all my goodness pass before thee, and I will proclaim the name of the LORD before thee; and will be gracious to whom I will be gracious, and will shew mercy on whom I will shew mercy."* As believers, we have witnessed more of the Glory of God than we realized. If you belong to God, you have seen, on numberless occasions, the Glory of God through His goodness (Exodus 33:8-9).

The psalmist David said, *"I will call upon the LORD, who is worthy to be praised..."* (Psalms 18:3). That is the cry of all Christians.

Week #18

THE ANSWER TO CURRENT WORLD EVENTS

The title of this article may seem to be bold and uninformed but, if we look to God's Word for understanding and knowledge, we can begin to see a fulfilling of God's Word in the current events the world is experiencing right now.

In John 14:29, Jesus said, *"And now I have told you before it come to pass, that, when it is come to pass, ye might believe."* The Prophet Isaiah tells us in Isaiah 13:13, *" Therefore I will shake the heavens, and the earth shall remove out of her place, in the wrath of the LORD of hosts, and in the day of his fierce anger."* Of this shaking, the Apostle Paul said in Hebrews 12:27, *"And this word, Yet once more, signifieth the removing of those things that are shaken, as of things that are made, that those things which cannot be shaken may remain."* The only things that will survive this shaking of God are those in the shelter of Him. When God told us of this time of shaking, He made it clear through Isaiah's words, it would include *"...the heavens, and the earth..."* that is everything and everyone. 2 Corinthians 5:11 says, *"Knowing therefore the terror of the Lord, we persuade men..."* Yes, believers know the terror of the Lord.

When God said in John 14:1, *"Let not your heart be troubled: ye believe in God, believe also in me"* because His children were afraid. There is fear even believers experience, but it is a righteous fear explained in Matthew 10:28 *"And fear not them which kill the body, but are not able to kill the soul: but rather fear him which is able to destroy both soul and body in hell."* That is the Word of God about our having the right kind of fear.

Today Christians are confused, and some have even denied the faith, but this is a time to raise up in the Name of the Lord and in the power of the Holy Ghost and give praise to our Conquering Lord (that) *"...in all these things we are more than conquerors through him that loved us"* (Romans 8:37).

We need a revival of repentance and forgiveness in the church, but what is happening in all nations of the world is not involving the church. It is a fulfillment of God's Word through many prophets that there would come a day of His vengeance against sin. This is what is happening before our eyes, from Isaiah 63:4, *"For the day of vengeance is in mine heart, and the year of my redeemed is come."* Isaiah 26:20 says, *"Come, my people, enter thou into thy chambers, and shut thy doors about thee: hide thyself as it were for a little moment until the indignation be overpast."* The Prophet Ezekiel says in addition to Isaiah, *"And I will execute great vengeance upon them with furious rebukes; and they shall know that I am the LORD, when I shall lay my vengeance upon them"* (Ezekiel 25:17). Further consider Isaiah 26:21 *"For, behold, the LORD cometh out of his place to punish the inhabitants of the earth for their iniquity: the earth also shall disclose her blood, and shall no more cover her slain."* Again, the Word of the Lord declares in Jeremiah 46:10, *"For this is the day of the Lord GOD of hosts, a day of vengeance, that he may avenge him of his adversaries: and the sword shall devour, and it shall be satiate and made drunk with their blood: for the Lord GOD of hosts hath a sacrifice in the north country by the river Euphrates."*

A precious and assuring word is given to every true child of God found in 1 Thessalonians 5:9, *"For God hath not appointed us to wrath, but to obtain salvation by our Lord Jesus Christ."* AMEN AND AMEN!

Week #19

WHEN GOD IS REJECTED

Decades ago, when the Bible and prayer were banned from schools many wondered what would become of our society – Now we know!

I received this timely message from a Christian family that I pastored for many years. It goes back to a decision made in America years ago. Godly Christians cried out against this rebellion against God and warned that there would be a price we would have to pay for turning our backs on God's Word. Our great God, who said in Amos 3:7, *"Surely the Lord GOD will do nothing, but he revealeth his secret unto his servants the prophets"* (messengers), is fulfilling His Holy Word. God gave warnings, through His Word, well in advance of this act against Him. In Psalms 9:17, when the writer said, *"The wicked shall be turned into hell, and all the nations that forget God,"* he was talking about hell being the nature of things in those nations before God came in His final judgment. The truth of this post is only evidence of the truth of God. It is a part of God's fulfilled Word, but unless America repents and turns to God, it is only the beginning of God's judgments dealing with this and all the nations of the earth. Individually, and as a nation, it is imperative that we humble ourselves and repent before God for our sins. He is merciful to forgive, and as He did with Israel, He will possibly repent Himself of His anger and spare a people. *"And the LORD repented of the evil which he thought to do unto his people."* (Exodus 32:14).

Isaiah 55:6-7 *" Seek ye the LORD while he may be found, call ye upon him while he is near: Let the wicked forsake his way, and the unrighteous man his thoughts: and let him return unto the LORD, and he will have mercy upon him; and to our God, for he will abundantly pardon. "* Now is the time. The door of His mercy remains open. I sound another warning from the Holy God found in Isaiah 66:4, *"I also will choose their delusions, and will bring their fears upon them; because when I called, none did answer; when I spake, they did not hear: but they did evil before mine eyes, and chose that in which I delighted not."*

Week #20

PEACE, SAFETY, AND DESTRUCTION

On September 28, 2020, I watched the signing of peace accords between the United States, Israel, and Bahrain. The Name of Jesus is *"...Prince of Peace"* (Isaiah 9:6). In John 14:27, Jesus tells His children, *" Peace I leave with you, my peace I give unto you: not as the world giveth, give I unto you. Let not your heart be troubled, neither let it be afraid."* It can be argued the greatest desire of man is peace and security. Wars are fought among nations to achieve peace, and individuals will stand alone in the face of attacks against themselves or families in the struggle for peace. I love and want peace, but real peace is not to be found in words and intentions. There is a foundation that lasting peace must be built upon, and the Supreme Commander (Jesus) that must agree to the terms and be satisfied by the terms set forth.

From the days of Abraham, the father of Ishmael and Isaac, when Abraham sent Ishmael (and his mother, Hagar) out from his tent at Sarah's request, the mother of Isaac, there has been and will continue to be a war between their dependents. Millenniums have passed since that event, but these two sons of Abraham nor their decedents will ever successfully reach a lasting peace. Kings and presidents, leaders of most nations, negotiators, and well-intentioned persons have sought an agreement among this divided family.

Why is this so important to speak about and understand? Because God said, there would come a day when this war, hatred, and division would seemingly change. Leaders and national officials would begin to say we want and have achieved PEACE. But God said in 1Thessalonians 5:3, *" For when they shall say, Peace and safety; then sudden destruction cometh upon them, as travail upon a woman with child; and they shall not escape."* Another attempt at achieving peace, another soon to be failure. For over 70 years, two peace accords have been signed by these relatives. Now, two more have been signed-in a single month. Other nations are said to be joining these accords soon. Many things can transpire before this prophecy is completed, but this is the time for the fulfillment of God to us.

I cannot give a time or a chronology of events, but I can speak from the Word of God. When Jesus was answering the question in Matthew 24 and 25 about times, seasons, and time of His return, He said this in Luke 21:28, *"And when these things begin to come to pass, then look up, and lift up your heads; for your redemption draweth nigh."* There have been myriads of peace accords through history, but the agreements today are noteworthy in Scripture. Jerusalem is known as the earth's navel, and every happening in it is important to all people. The reference in 1 Thessalonians is a prime example of what will come out of these accords. Jesus is to return to this earth very, very, very soon. BE READY!

The question can and should be asked about the soon appearing of Jesus to earth again. We read Jesus' reply to those who asked Him that question from Matthew 24:36 *" But of that day and hour knoweth no man, no, not the angels of heaven, but my Father only."* Everyone must ask for forgiveness of sins, pray, live clean before God, and watch for His glorious return.

Week #21

GUILT BY ASSOCIATION

Regrettably, there is an indifference to the Word of God in the world and church today. This indifference has fostered and created an ignorance of the important issues of life. This must be overcome by a sincere and prayerful reading and studying of the Bible. It is the only Book of Life. No matter how educated an individual is, he is not fully educated until he is educated in God's Word.

2 Corinthians 13:5 tells everyone, *"Examine yourselves, whether ye be in the faith; prove your own selves. Know ye not your own selves, how that Jesus Christ is in you, except ye be reprobates?"* A close examination of what we believe and why, our lifestyles, associates, our motives, etc. will reveal many things that are hard to deal with. In the long run, if we will repent of our failures and waywardness, it will be the best experience of our lives. When this examination reveals the real us that we did not know was there, it brings a thorough cleansing of spirit, soul, body, and mind: what a change and a personal relief.

A truth that most people never think of is how God sees us. We are told we will give an account of our actions and ways of whether they were good or bad (2 Corinthians 5:10). God will judge everything about me and you. In Romans 1:32, we see we will be viewed according to what was a pleasure to us, *" Who knowing the judgment of God, that they which commit such things are worthy of death, not only do the same, but have pleasure in them that do them."* The word "pleasure" here means to give approval to those who have committed wickedness against God. Romans 1:18 says, *"...the wrath of God is revealed from heaven against all ungodliness and unrighteousness of men, who hold the truth in unrighteousness."* In verse 21, he names such sins as not glorifying God, being unthankful to God, becoming vain in their imaginations, and having foolish hearts. In verse 22, He identifies falsely claiming wisdom, yet being fools. Verse 23 adds they changed the glory of God and the truth of God unto a lie. Then in verse 25, He said they worshipped the creature instead of Him, the Creator.

The Apostle Paul asked in 2 Corinthians 6:15, *"And what concord hath Christ with Belial?"* (the spirit of evil personified; the devil; Satan), *"or what part hath he that believeth with an infidel?"* A true believer has no part with an infidel.

As an example, and volumes could be written to add to this one matter, I recently heard the latest statistics on abortions in America is 100 million. I cannot be a part of those that would kill the unborn. I know those who destroy these babies will be judged, sentenced to die the wicked's death. Based on the penalty of God defined in Romans 1:32, I cannot support anyone guilty of abortion.

We need to let God turn His searchlight on even the most secret parts of our minds and hearts. If we do not permit it now by our free choice, it will be done in judgment by His choosing.

Week #22

SOWING SEEDS IN TIME OF FLOOD

A very familiar Old Testament Scripture is the first verse of Ecclesiastes 11:1, *"Cast thy bread upon the waters: for thou shalt find it after many days."* This verse is usually interpreted to be confined to the rich giving to the poor. I do not question this interpretation but believe it includes more truth.

Bible teachers agree the region that is spoken of here is along the Nile River. The reference to bread is actually "seeds" planted for food crops, and the waters are in reference to the Nile River. Most Egyptian cities along this body of water and their civilization depended on the Nile River and its seasonal flooding. This flooding was an annual event, and the Egyptians used it to have a significant agriculture industry.

When the river flooded, it covered the land with rich soil from the river bottom. Where the ground had been arid and dry, and it was difficult to raise crops, this seasonal flooding made the ground very fertile. While the Nile was still in flood stage, the workers would spread the crop seeds on top of the water. When the waters receded, the seeds were then planted in the very rich soil taken from the river's bottom.

There is no doubt about those that have helped to meet the needs of others by giving. This act of "casting your bread upon the waters" affects people's futures. In our time with all that is available to help us reach people, yes with, but not limited to food, how much more should we that have the everlasting Gospel, be casting our bread upon the waters of the lives of multitudes in need of God.

Jesus said in Matthew 10:8, *"...freely ye have received, freely give."* I believe masses of people would believe the Gospel and come to Christ if we would sow the seed. If you love Christ and those He died for, who have never received this good news, I ask you to pray and consider helping those who are called to *"Go ye into all the world, and preach the gospel to every creature"* (Mark 16:15).

Week #23

A MOST IMPORTANT DECISION

Peter tells us how God communicated His Word to us in 2 Peter 1:21 saying, *"For the prophecy* (the revealed Word) *came not in old time by the will of man: but holy men of God spake as they were moved by the Holy Ghost."* In the previous verse, the Apostle says, by the Holy Spirit, *"Knowing this first, that no prophecy* (message) *of the scripture is of any private interpretation"* (2 Peter 1:20). God's Holy Spirit reveals the Mind of God in all matters given His will in the Bible. These two verses tell us how Scripture was given and how it was to be rightly used and followed.

The Eternal God commanded in Deuteronomy 4:2, *"Ye shall not add unto the word which I command you, neither shall ye diminish ought from it, that ye may keep the commandments of the LORD your God which I command you."* In Revelation 22:18-19, God reveals the eternal punishment for breaking His commandments when He said, *"For I testify unto every man that heareth the words of the prophecy* (message) *of this book, If any man shall add unto these things,* (the Word of God), *God shall add unto him the plagues that are written in this book: And if any man shall take away from the words of the book of this prophecy* (message), *God shall take away his part out of the book of life, and out of the holy city, and from the things which are written in this book."* Biblical plagues and eternal separation from God are the judgments of God for this sin.

On any given subject, one man's opinion is of no more value than that of another man. God's Word is not an opinion. He said in Isaiah 55:11, *"So shall my word be that goeth forth out of my mouth: it shall not return unto me void, but it shall accomplish that which I please, and it shall prosper in the thing whereto I sent it."*

With this truth established, the Word of the Lord is forever settled, it shall never fail, and it abides forever. Further, *"...let God be true, but every man a liar..."* says the Apostle Paul (Romans 3:4).

I have convictions, based on the Word of God that I feel compelled to address. In a matter of days, our country will have an election. I try to speak of things securely rooted in the Bible and not opinion. What I will say is spoken on those safe and secure grounds. I will in no way be political, but scriptural, in speaking to these issues.

It is estimated that over 100 million babies have been aborted in America. The Bible is not silent on this subject. I have spoken to women who had an abortion, repented, and forgiven for this crime. I will give scriptural references, where God has spoken about abortion. He said, *"Thou shalt not kill"* (Exodus 20:13). Exodus 21:22-25 states, *"f men strive, and hurt a woman with child, so that her fruit depart from her, and yet no mischief follow: he shall be surely punished, according as the woman's husband will lay upon him; and he shall pay as the judges determine. And if any mischief follow, then thou shalt give life for life, Eye for eye, tooth for tooth, hand for hand, foot for foot, Burning for burning, wound for wound, stripe for stripe."* America is facing the judgment of God.

The Almighty knew each of these innocent babies, and even called them by name as found in Isaiah 49:1 *"...The LORD hath called me from the womb; from the bowels of my mother hath he made mention of my name."*

David said in Psalms 139:13-16 *"For thou hast possessed my reins: thou hast covered me in my mother's womb. I will praise thee; for I am fearfully and wonderfully made: marvellous are thy works; and that my soul knoweth right well. My substance was not hid from thee, when I was made in secret, and curiously wrought in the lowest parts of the earth. Thine eyes did see my substance, yet being unperfect; and in thy book all my members were written, which in continuance were fashioned, when as yet there was none of them."*

Christians cannot go against the Word of the Lord. Those who run for elected office may not be saved, but their position on things spoken of in the Bible makes us accountable for how we respond in supporting them.

This is a critical time for our nation, but it is a more critical time for professing Christians. If a political party is contrary to God's Word, we must stand against personal opinions and personalities, and take a strong Biblical and fearful stand for our Savior.

Week #24

MY PRAYER FOR YOU

Everyone who prays and believes is thankful for this promise from God in 1 John 5:14-15, *"And this is the confidence that we have in him, that, if we ask anything according to his will, he heareth us: And if we know that he hear us, whatsoever we ask, we know that we have the petitions that we desired of him."* The Apostle Peter said in 2 Peter 3:9, *"The Lord is not slack concerning his promise...,"* that is to say that whatever He says He fulfills. God answers prayer. We are to pray about everything and everyone. In Matthew 5:44-45, the Lord says to us, *"But I say to you, love your enemies, bless them that curse you, do good to them that hate you, and pray for them which despitefully use you, and persecute you; That ye may be the children of your Father which is in heaven: for he maketh his sun to rise on the evil and on the good, and sendeth rain on the just and on the unjust."* That may be hard to do, but it is the will of God. We are also instructed to pray that ministers and laborers would take the Gospel to the whole world. In Matthew 9:36-38, it says, *"But when he saw the multitudes, he was moved with compassion on them, because they fainted, and were scattered abroad, as sheep having no shepherd. Then saith he unto his disciples, The harvest truly is plenteous, but the labourers are few; Pray ye therefore the Lord of the harvest, that he will send forth labourers into his harvest."* In the Gospel of Luke chapter 21 and verse 36 Jesus says, *"Watch ye therefore, and pray always, that ye may be accounted worthy to escape all these things that shall come to pass, and to stand before the Son of man."*

There is no experience like prayer. We speak to the Father, and He, in turn, speaks to us. His unfailing promise is, *"If ye abide in me, and my words abide in you, ye shall ask what ye will, and it shall be done unto you"* (John 15:7). When we pray, 1 Thessalonians 5:17 says, *"Pray without ceasing."* We read in Philippians 4:6 to *"Be careful for nothing; but in every thing by prayer and supplication with thanksgiving let your requests be made known unto God."* We should pray the Will of God, of which we named a few, but we also are to approach God in prayer to "make our petitions known." I thank God for the opportunity to share these posts with you. I pray for you. Very briefly, because of available space, my prayer to God for you includes *"Brethren, my heart's desire and prayer to God for (you) Israel is, that they might be saved"* (Romans 10:1). And lastly, from Numbers 6:24-26, *"The Lord bless thee, and keep thee: The Lord make his face shine upon thee, and be gracious unto thee: The Lord lift up his countenance upon thee, and give thee peace."* Amen!

Week #25

MERCY: NOT GETTING THE PUNISHMENT WE DESERVE

"...the LORD your God is gracious and merciful, and will not turn away his face from you, if ye return unto him" (2 Chronicles 30:9).

The occasion of the 51st Psalm is the sin of David with Bathsheba. David slept with Bathsheba, who was another man's wife. Uriah, her husband, was a faithful soldier of David. David had him slain in battle for the express purpose of taking his wife. Others were also killed, and many other criminal activities were done. David showed no evidence of being sorry for what he had done but continued on his way until he was confronted by a Holy man of God by the name of Nathan. This Holy man was sent by God to David to expose his sin. David immediately repented and prayed that he would receive mercy from God. David wrote this Psalm about his wicked deeds, and God preserved it as a permanent record about sin, repentance, and God's directions about how to be forgiven. This record gives every sinner instructions, for every sin, how to go humbly to God for help.

Many times David prayed for the mercies of God to come to him. He did not try to hide his guilt or blame something or someone else; he cried for the mercy of God. He did not want to be cast away from God but to gain mercy and be accepted into the favor of the Lord. His prayer is recorded in Psalms 51:1; *"...Have mercy upon me, O God, according to thy lovingkindness: according unto the multitude of thy tender mercies blot out my transgressions."* He knew how wretched he was and that God was the source of mercy and his help. He did not stand in his past accomplishments and heroic acts. He threw himself on the love of God. 1 John 4:8 says, *"...God is love."* Mercy comes from love.

In Psalm 51:2, David asks to be thoroughly cleaned. He wants to be washed from the wickedness and sin that was upon him as a result of his sin. His conscience condemned him. He had lived with this guilt and now sincerely desired to be clean. He acknowledged his sin. He confessed his sin. He repented of his sin. God hates sin, and he punishes unrepentant sinners and has prepared a place of eternal punishment for those who do not come to Him for deliverance.

To all who have sinned, any manner of sin, follow David's example. Confess: *"For I acknowledge my transgressions: and my sin is ever before me."* Go to Him for mercy, as David did in Psalms 51. The God of love and mercy will fulfill this promise to all who ask of Him, *"For thou, Lord, art good, and ready to forgive: and plenteous in mercy unto all them that call upon thee"* (Psalms 86:5).

Week #26

SORROW AND GRIEF

The prophet Isaiah said Jesus *was "... a man of sorrows, and acquainted with grief..."* (Isaiah 53:3). Have you seriously considered these words? I have, but I do not believe our human understanding and limited vocabulary can, in any measure, comprehend the depths of these words. Jesus said in Luke 22:44, *"And being in an agony he prayed more earnestly: and his sweat was as it were great drops of blood falling down to the ground."* His sorrow and grief started before His crucifixion had begun. I can speak only briefly to this statement. Was it because His dearest friends were leaving and betraying Him? Was it the realization of physical suffering and going to the heart of the earth and meeting Satan? Jesus is Lord. As wicked men led Him to Calvary, He declared, *"...Destroy this temple, and in three days I will raise it up"* (John 2:19). So, what could be the source of His sorrows and grief? It was more likely the unbearable, in His earthly body, the burden of bearing all mankind's sins to come for thousands of years. As He took this sin, He knew the Father would turn His back on Him as He became the sin sacrifice for all of Adam's race.

The Word of God assures us in John 16:33, *"These things I have spoken unto you, that in me ye might have peace. In the world ye shall have tribulation: but be of good cheer; I have overcome the world."* The Bible is a spiritual book about Christ. It is not to be used outside of that truth. *"So God created man in his own image, in the image of God created he him; male and female created he them"* (Genesis 1:27). But from the book of Hebrews 2:14, we see, *"Forasmuch then as the children are partakers of flesh and blood..."* we must deal and overcome ours in our natural bodies. Thank God 1 John

3:2 telling us, *"Beloved, now are we the sons of God, and it doth not yet appear what we shall be: but we know that, when he shall appear, we shall be like him; for we shall see him as he is."* What a glorious promise. When we see Him, we shall be like Him. Exactly what God's intention for us was in the beginning.

The King James Bible Dictionary gives a partial definition of sorrow as "The uneasiness or pain of mind which is produced by the loss of any good or of frustrated hopes of good, or expected loss of happiness; to grieve; to be sad."

Many sorrows are mentioned in Scripture that is common to us. Barren women sorrowed for want of children. Parents sorrowed over rebellious and lost children. We all have lost loved ones etc. and know these are reasons to be sad. God gives comfort no matter the cause of our need.

God's promise to His people is found in Revelation 21:4, *"And God shall wipe away all tears from their eyes; and there shall be no more death, neither sorrow, nor crying, neither shall there be any more pain: for the former things are passed away."*

Week #27

THE BLESSED

On July 4, 2020, we, as a nation, celebrated Independence Day. This day is accepted as the birthday of our great Republic. Our country was 244 years old on that day. We thank God for His limitless blessings to The United States of America. All real Americans offer our gratitude to the countless multitudes that paid a personal, and even their very lives, toward the national greatness and independence of this land. We honor and recognize those who, through military service and any other methods, contributed to making this the greatest nation. Besides thanking Almighty God, we honor the Christians and Christian patriots who have contributed so much to this God-blessed nation through prayer, giving, and sacrifice.

There is also a spiritual need before this world and the believer's responsibility to it. Deliverance, freedom from sin, and eternal damnation are the most urgent needs for everyone of any generation. Jesus Christ has paid the price for every soul to have peace, joy, and everlasting life. He paid all the costs, and He now has called for every recipient of His salvation to tell everyone else of His love and salvation to all who will repent of their sin and be born again. Scripture says in John 8:36, *"If the Son therefore shall make you free, ye shall be free indeed."* Following our personal salvation experience with Christ, we are directed and instructed to become witness' for the Lord. That is our call and mandate. Not just a call for a preacher, but every born-again believer is called to tell their families, strangers, and even their enemies of God's love for them and share the Gospel message of God's forgiveness. To be instrumental in helping a sinner to Christ is the greatest happiness in an individual's life. To know that it was by our truthful witness of Christ, a person has exchanged a life of eternal damnation for an eternal life with Jesus is beyond all other pleasures.

America and all other nations are going to pass away (Mark 13:31). God said in 2 Peter 3:13, *"Nevertheless we, according to His promise, look for new heavens and a new earth, wherein dwelleth righteousness."* When He returns, we will never have another opportunity to tell this great Gospel story. We must work while it is still day. My prayer is that God will revive and stir His people to again pray for and witness to those who are perishing without God's love.

Week #28

THE ANTICHRIST

It would take volumes of books to properly and adequately address this Bible subject. In a few words, I will give a few Scriptural truths about this man, who, in his time, is to be revealed.

First, what is meant by the prefix "anti?" One meaning is "the instead of Christ." This evil man will be a substitute for Christ. 2 Thessalonians, chapter 2:3 & 8, shows how he will impersonate the real Christ. In chapter 4, the antichrist will claim to be god. This wicked one will come in place of Christ. He is the devil's counterpart and impersonator of Christ.

In his deceiving attempt to imitate and replace the real Christ, this man of sin hates Jesus Christ and His children. In Revelation 12, he is represented by the dragon who pursues the church's representative described as a woman. (A sincere study into these stated facts will become more apparent and further evidence of his intended deception and destruction). The antichrist "the instead of Christ" against the church is revealed in Revelation, chapter 13: 3, as one "wondered after" by the entire world. In Revelations 13:7, it reads, *"And it was given unto him to make war with the saints, and to overcome them: and power was given him over all kindreds, and tongues, and nations."*

Thoughtful consideration of political and spiritual events in the world today gives crystal clear evidence of the antichrist's reality at work. John said in 1 John 2:18, *"Little children, it is the last time: and as ye have heard that antichrist shall come, even now are there many antichrists; whereby we know that it is the last time."*

Yes, the spirit of the antichrist is in the world through his followers, believers, and workers, but it is foretold in 2 Thessalonians 2:3 of the antichrist personal appearing thusly, *"...that man of sin be revealed, the son of perdition."*

The real Christ came in love, but the antichrist will be the personification of hate. Christ was, and is, in-dwelt by the Spirit of God. The antichrist will be filled with the spirit of Satan. Christ came to save, and the antichrist came to damn.

The ruin and destruction wrought by the antichrist will be unfathomable. It does not have to be that way for you. God cast the devil, and his fallen angels, out of heaven. He sent His Son to redeem all who would believe and accept His great salvation. Read and study the Word of God. Call upon the Lord for the forgiveness of sins. That way, you will not be deceived by the spirit of deception and be lost. Pray as did Paul in Philippians 3:10-*11* *"That I may know him, and the power of his resurrection, and the fellowship of his sufferings, being made conformable unto his death; If by any means I might attain unto the resurrection of the dead."*

Week #29

FAITH

The 11th chapter of the book of Hebrews is called the Hall of Faith chapter of the Bible. It has been said that The Hall of Faith demonstrates that faith enables us and others to do many great things for the Lord. It teaches us that we can do anything through and by faith, and nothing is impossible with God. Indeed, verse one of Hebrews 11 says, *"Now faith is the substance of things hoped for, the evidence of things not seen."* Faith is the answer to what is not only hope and invisible to our natural sight. But faith gives the believer confidence in the reality of what he expects by faith. In Hebrews 11, many verses speak of *"through faith"* and *"by faith."* Both of these statements mean "because of faith."

When it comes to thoughts about the Church's future and the promise of God to it, many have spiritually thrown up their hands and surrendered to a feeling of utter helplessness and hopelessness. We need to return to faith and confidence in God that He is all-knowing and all-powerful, and He will, without doubt, honor and fulfill every jot and tittle of His never changing or unfailing Word.

Some, even professing Christians, have no confidence in God's promises. I believe one reason for this is the Bible is just words to them. But a man or woman of faith believes, unreservedly, all Scripture because it is in their heart, not only their minds.

The Church has gone and will continue to go through every attack the devil will unsuccessfully, for the true believer and person of faith, put it through until Jesus comes for His children. Until the resurrection, the believer has the eternal Word of God to stand on against the devil's wiles and overcome his deceptions and fightings.

Every promise God has made is for you and me. Every one of us individually. Be strong in the Lord. Pray and read the Bible. Carefully study the Word. Repent and be cleansed from sin and unbelief. Have faith in God. He has already won the battle against the devil and hell and has shared this victory with His Church. *"Let not your heart be troubled: ye believe in God, believe also in me"* (John 14:1).

Week #30

WHY ME?

Each life is lived individually, yet many questions in life are common to everyone. This includes questions that come in challenging or difficult times. Questions such as "why me," or "what did I do to deserve this," or "I have no idea where that came from," or even "I would never have believed that person would say that about me or turn on me like this?" We tend to isolate experiences in life that, in reality, are not without a connection to some other happening in our past.

I once heard my pastor say, "if you don't like someone, don't worry about it because there is someone that does not like you." We need to be reminded that Romans 14:7 says, *"For none of us liveth to himself, and no man dieth to himself."* One meaning of this is what you do affects someone else, and what others do can affect you.

For the most part, we find fault with other people and blame them for any differences we may have. When in reality, we need first to examine ourselves. It may require serious thinking and searching of our lives to reach the true reason things have worked out this particular way. Can it be that Galatians 6:7 has been fulfilled in me (that*) "...whatsoever a man soweth, that shall he also reap."* Have I actually contributed to this issue and, until now, I had forgotten what I had said or what I had done.

The fact is disputed, and separations come to all of us. I can't control what another person says and does, but I can control what I say or do going forward. I can ask God to forgive me. I can ask others to forgive me. I can let the misunderstanding go and not hold the difference I had with someone else any longer. Why and how? Because when I contributed to the overall situation, I did not take time to remember Galatians 6:7.

Since this truth is so much larger than this simple example and can be approached from differing viewpoints, the Biblical truth always remains, be mindful of what you say and do because you may be faced with it again. I pray that we all would love one another according to John 13:34 *"A new commandment I give unto you, That ye love one another; as I have loved you, that ye also love one another."* Jesus took this love to include this commandment in Matthew 5:44 *"But I say unto you, Love your enemies, bless them that curse you, do good to them that hate you, and pray for them which despitefully use you, and persecute you."*

In all that we do and say, remember this rule of "sowing and reaping."

Week #31

TRIFLING INCIDENTS HAVE BIG EFFECTS

The radio voice of the Assemblies of God Fellowship worldwide radio ministry "Revivaltime" was C. M. Ward. In his message entitled "Darts of Death," he recounted this testimony.

"Death is a process... History is an auditor's report that tells us that trifling incidents have significant effects, and here is an example. A Chinese youth had attended a mission's school where his western teachers much admired him. Several years after he had left the missions school, he heard that his beloved friend had returned to visit the city where he had formerly taught. Eagerly the young man made his way to the large motel where the missionary was staying, and the doorman refused to admit him. But the determined young Chinese man managed to make his way to the lobby where he explained his mission. Get out said the clerk. But I want to see my teacher; he's a missionary. I don't care if he is a missionary said the clerk; we do not want Chinese around here. Then the slight young Chinese man was escorted out of the hotel by a big westerner. The student never forgot. It did not matter that he had been educated for a time in a western school or that his teacher whom he had admired was a westerner. The young man believed that the way real westerners behaved was like the men at the hotel. He was humiliated and never forgot the experience. What happened to that young Chinese man at the hands of that westerner that day is something upon which we may reflect with irony for the name of that young man was Mao Tse-tung" (Mao Zedong). The "trifling" experience he had in a hotel played some part in the effects of his life in the world. Taught for a time

74

by a western missionary, he became responsible for humanity's most deaths ever.

Sometimes, even seemingly, most insignificant actions can involve one soul or countless numbers of souls. In a Washington Post article by Ilya Somin dated August 3, 2016, Chairman Mao ..." was the biggest mass murderer in the history of the world. ...From 1958 to 1962, his Great Leap Forward policy led to up to 45 million people's deaths.

Dr. Ward reported he was affected and offended by a doorman and a clerk in a hotel as a young Chinese student. Of course, this is like no other story in history, but the lesson to be learned is how our actions affect other people.

Isaiah 43:10 says, *"Ye [are] my witnesses, saith the LORD..."* Jesus encouraged His disciples to *"Let your light so shine before men, that they may see your good works, and glorify your Father which is in heaven"* in Matthew 5:16. In Acts 1:8, Luke says by the Holy Spirit, *"...ye shall be witnesses unto me both in Jerusalem, and in all Judaea, and in Samaria, and unto the uttermost part of the earth."*

Since we are *"...epistle was written in our hearts, known and read of all men,"* found in 2 Corinthians 3:2, let us bear witness of the loving care of Jesus Christ. Let us all remember, "Trifling Incidents have Big Effects."

(C. M. Ward – (1909-2007) Pastor, Evangelist, Revivaltime radio broadcaster 1953-1978.)

Week #32

COMPROMISE

I recently traded in my seven-year-old car. Mileage and other factors entered into the decision to change vehicles. This was during the coronavirus pandemic, and there was a shortage of vehicles to choose from. A person had to pick some things they otherwise would have dismissed and do without other items they would have desired to have on a car. I told the sales staff this was a trying experience, but they and I had to compromise to settle on a vehicle.

After all of our discussion, I thought about those who have compromised their beliefs, convictions, and standing with God. It is one thing to compromise in life's business decisions, but another when it involves eternal matters. Possessions will decay and one day be replaced. God never changes, diminishes, or is replaced. He never changes, as seen in Malachi 3:6a, *"For I am the LORD, I change not..."*

Aaron, the brother of Moses, had witnessed all the miracles that God had worked for the children of Israel. He had seen the Red Sea parted, how God protected them with a cloud and a fire, gave heavenly food to eat, and they drank water out of a rock. While Moses was meeting with God, Aaron compromised with the people. They made a golden calf, gave it credit for bringing them out of their troubles, and worshiped it as a god.

Aaron was a leader of the people, but he was undoubtedly swayed by the people who had other ideas about what was the right way to proceed other than Moses's ways. Repeatedly the Bible says that as God led Moses, he led the people. They needed a leader that would not compromise the ways of God. Aaron was not as strong as Moses to resist the ways of the natural man and solely obey and follow God.

Today many leaders have compromised the right way, followed the desires of human thinking, and spiritually built their own golden calf. It has been rightly said that most people want a "user-friendly" religion with no interference from a Godly leader or God Himself. They want to be left alone in their godly shortcomings and be ushered straight into heaven. In Exodus, God showed His anger toward this condition. Only the prayer of Moses for the people changed God's mind toward them. We need Godly, uncompromising leaders to pray for us and faithfully show us the things and ways of God.

Moses loved these people so much that he was willing even to be blotted out by God for them. Rather than destroying these people for their error, Moses prayed for his brother and all of the people.

Refuse to compromise the ways of God and find faithful, strong, and uncompromising leaders that will love you, pray for you, discipline you, even to the point they will be willing to face separation from God to see you in complete fellowship with God. Refuse compromise.

Week #33

THE NAME ABOVE ALL NAMES

I begin this post with great carefulness. My subject is Deity, Who is eternal, beyond measure, indescribable, of which no human can do more than attempt to speak about Him. Jesus Christ, the Son of God. I pray that God will be pleased with my effort to share a few Biblical truths concerning His Son and that I will not mislead or speak falsely. For me, this is a significant undertaking. I hope everyone understands my heartfelt seriousness in speaking of Jesus.

Many people say Jesus was named by an angel based on Matthew 1:20-21. The angel announced His coming, but God named His Only Son. In Philippians 2:9-11, the Apostle Paul says of the naming of Jesus, *"Wherefore God also hath highly exalted him, and given him a name which is above every name: That at the name of Jesus every knee should bow, of things in heaven, and things in earth, and things under the earth; And that every tongue should confess that Jesus Christ is Lord, to the glory of God the Father."*

In the Bible, the indescribable One is given titles and descriptions to help our human understanding. He is called or referred to as, Master, the Son of God, Son of man, Son of David, Lamb of God, the Last Adam, Light of the World, the King of the Jews, Rabbi, Savior, the Chosen One, the I Am, Apostle, High Priest, Prophet Priest and King, Faithful and True, Alpha and Omega and the Morning Star. That is only a sampling of the revealed names and titles given concerning Jesus Christ.

One author said, "...Jesus is not a some system of a doctrine about Him... or just what we believe concerning

Him... The truth and testimony of Jesus is what He... is what He…is in Himself in the eyes of God."

In Matthew 16:13-17, Jesus asked Peter *"...Whom do men say that I the Son of man am?"* to which Peter answered, *"Thou art the Christ, the Son of the living God."* Jesus assured Peter this was a natural recognition of Him but was Divinely given by the *"...Father which is in heaven."*

That is the only way to know Jesus Christ. As earlier stated in this post, it is not human understanding, beliefs, doctrines, and personal opinions. When a person asks of God to be given a true and Divine revelation of Jesus Christ, the Father Who is no respecter of persons (Romans 2:11). The never-failing promise of Jesus to everyone is in John 5:24 *"Verily, verily, I say unto you, He that heareth my word, and believeth on him that sent me, hath everlasting life, and shall not come into condemnation; but is passed from death unto life."* In John 12:21, some people asked to see Jesus. According to the eternal Word of God, if anyone will, *"Delight thyself also in the LORD; and he shall give thee the desires of thine heart"* (Psalms 37:4).

We do not only want to know about Jesus; we want to know Jesus.

Week #34

FUTURE WORLD

Certain Scripture brings a Holy fear to my ministerial life. One such verse is Deuteronomy 18:20, *"But the prophet, which shall presume to speak a word in my name, which I have not commanded him to speak, or that shall speak in the name of other gods, even that prophet shall die."* I fear God as referenced in Proverbs 1:7, *"The fear of the Lord is the beginning of knowledge..."* Based entirely on what I believe to be the undisputed truth of God's never-failing Word, I want to share this thought I have entitled "Future World." This is not a prophecy but the stated Words of Jesus Christ. These are the coming events to the entire world, including America.

Jesus said in Matthew 24:37, *"But as the days of Noah were, so shall also the coming of the Son of man be."* Hopefully, everyone reading this knows that God destroyed the earth with a flood in Noah's time. This same God has promised to do it again. 2 Peter 3:10 reads, *"But the day of the Lord will come as a thief in the night; in the which the heavens shall pass away with a great noise, and the elements shall melt with fervent heat, the earth also and the works that are therein shall be burned up."* Knowing this will come in God's time, the question is, what was it like in the days of Noah? Thankfully God has told us what He wants us to know, and it is sufficient to give a warning and a way to escape these unbelievable days.

I will furnish Scriptural references and let the Word of God be the speaker. In 2 Timothy 3 verses 1-4, some of these verses describe *"...perilous times, men who are covetous, blasphemers, disobedient to parents, unthankful, unholy, without natural affections, trucebreakers, false accusers, fierce, despisers of those that were good, traitors, heady, highminded, lovers of pleasure more than lovers of God."* These references speak of what it will be like in the time of the end spoken in connection with Noah's time.

Genesis 6:5 says of Noah's time, *"And God saw that the wickedness of man was great in the earth, and that every imagination of the thoughts of his heart was only evil continually."* Verses 11-12 of that same chapter reads, *"The earth also was corrupt before God, and the earth was filled with violence. And God looked upon the earth, and, behold, it was corrupt; for all flesh had corrupted his way upon the earth."* Jesus said in Luke 17:26-27, *"And as it was in the days of Noe, so shall it be also in the days of the Son of man. They did eat, they drank, they married wives, they were given in marriage, until the day that Noah entered into the ark, and the flood came, and destroyed them all."* In Genesis 6:6, God said of this condition of man, *"And it repented the Lord that he had made man on the earth, and it grieved him at his heart."* There came a day of judgment for every person not in Noah's ark of safety, and a day will come when everyone not in Christ, our ark of safety, will be destroyed. This is the future of the world. In several Bible references, we read, as in Numbers 23:19, *"God is not a man, that he should lie; neither the Son of man, that he should repent: hath he said, and shall he not do it? or hath he spoken, and shall he not make it good?"* These days are coming, and I believe very soon.

These verses cover a wide span of time, but God is not measured by time. 2 Peter 3:8 says, *"But, beloved, be not ignorant of this one thing, that one day is with the Lord as a thousand years, and a thousand years as one day."* It will happen just as He declared it.

Noah lived 1600 years after Adam and Eve. As I write this, it is January 20, 2021. According to man's measurement of time, that is a long time, but God looks at it differently.

Continents, nations, cities, and people, either rich or poor, are experiencing common troubles. This is not an isolated phenomenon but is so generally common everywhere that only God can bring man to either be saved or be judged for his sin. In Noah's day, there were giants in the land (Genesis 6:4). Today there are giants in the land; we call them tech giants. They are influencing and working their wickedness as much as the literal giants in Noah's day.

Please remember the spoken Word of God from Luke 17:26, *"And as it was in the days of Noe, so shall it be also in the days of the Son of man"*. Thank God for the Biblical account of the end of these "...days of Noah..." and the end of the "...days of the Son of man..."

Genesis 6:8 says, *"BUT NOAH FOUND GRACE IN THE EYES OF THE LORD."* Noah and his wife had three sons, and they each had wives. Noah received the grace of God, as did his wife, his sons, and his daughters-in-law. The conditions outside the ark of safety could not touch them. They were both safe and secure. God has a place of safety and security in our day also. It is to be found in Christ. Repent of all sin, live faithfully and completely for Christ, and you will share this testimony with Noah and his family. We will overcome in Jesus' Name. Amen!

Week #35

DEFINING THE FINAL JUDGMENT

In obedience to and in the spirit of Ephesians 4:15 to *"...speaking the truth in love..."* I post this sobering thought about the final judgment. I offer it in love and concern for everyone. Hebrews 9:27 assures everyone *"And as it is appointed unto men once to die, but after this the judgment:"* 2 Corinthians 5:10 reads, *"For we must all appear before the judgment seat of Christ; that every one may receive the things done in his body, according to that he hath done, whether it be good or bad."*

From the verse in 2 Corinthians, we know exactly what this judgment will be. No surprises. No false charges and no lying witnesses. Just God on His high and lofty throne along with you and me and our life's testimony. We see the proof of this in the Book of Revelation chapter 20 and verse 12, *"And I saw the dead, small and great, stand before God; and the books were opened: and another book was opened, which is the book of life: and the dead were judged out of those things which were written in the books, according to their works."*

It is me and my life's testimony—nothing of anyone else. Just me with my record being read to me for which I must give an account before the Eternal, all-knowing God. Line by line, every action, deed, word, etc., will be made known. This judgment is not for God to know; He is already all-knowing. The exposure is for my sentencing, whether to life everlasting or a place in an eternal hell. It is all based on the record of the things I have done in my lifetime and not one thing more. To the Christian, I admonish you to *"...lay aside every weight, and the sin which doth so easily beset us..."* (Hebrews 12:1). To any poor unsaved soul I plead, do not run from conviction, for that conviction is the *"...godly sorrow (that) worketh repentance to salvation..."* (2 Corinthians 7:10). Romans 10:13 says of God's mercy to lost souls is *"For whosoever shall call upon the name of the Lord shall be saved."* You are going to be at the judgment seat, either saved or lost to eternal life or eternal death. Write in the testimony of your life and let it be read on that great and notable day that you repented of sin and received God's reward of eternal life. Hear the Word of the Lord.

Week #36

PRAY FOR ME

There are about eight times in Scripture where the Apostle Paul speaks about the need for prayer for himself. In reality, it might be more accurate to say that Paul "told" people to pray for him. In most instances, he gave the reason for this urgent need for prayer. I want to look to this great man, if God's asking for others to pray for him, I or most others, would not dare compare their lives to this man, but every other individual and I need others to pray on our behalf.

In the epistle of James chapter 5 and verse 16, the apostle gives this exhortation "...pray one for another..." On the same subject of praying for others, Paul said in 1 Timothy 2:1, *"I exhort therefore, that, first of all, supplications, prayers, intercessions, [and] giving of thanks, be made for all men."* Again, an exhortation from Paul in Ephesians 6:18 says, *"Praying always with all prayer and supplication in the Spirit, and watching thereunto with all perseverance and supplication for all saints."*

As stated earlier, the apostle, at times, gave a reason for requesting prayer. I will make this my request, without being too specific, because I need God's help, leadership, wisdom, and guidance, along with so many other such needs. I once was preaching revival for a pastor that said a minister should never request prayer from a church because he was supposed to be above such needs of prayer. I silently rejected that advice then and now reaffirm my continuing rejection by asking everyone for prayer on my behalf. The last time I heard anyone speak of him was to say that he had gone away from God. I don't know that for sure, but if so, he would have undoubtedly been helped by the prayers of people who would have lifted him to God in sincere prayer.

Thank God that the reason for my asking people to lift me up in prayer is that He will grant me everything I need as I love Him, walk with Him, submit myself to Him until the day I hear my loving Savior say, *"...Well done, thou good and faithful servant: thou hast been faithful over a few things, I will make thee ruler over many things: enter thou into the joy of thy lord"* (Matthew 25:21).

Week #37

A GROANING CREATION

Hold on! Don't stop reading yet. I have not yet completed my words for you. The Bible has the final word on everything, even in this troubling and evil day. But we must look at the total picture, so please continue reading. I have good news. God said in Romans 8:22-23, *"For we know that the whole creation groaneth and travaileth in pain together until now. And not only they, but ourselves also, which have the firstfruits of the Spirit, even we ourselves groan within ourselves, waiting for the adoption, to wit, the redemption of our body."* Groaning is the condition everywhere and in every life. Webster's 1828 Dictionary defines groan as "To breathe with a deep murmuring sound; to utter a mournful voice, as in pain or sorrow. To sigh; to be oppressed or afflicted, or to complain of oppression. A nation groans under the weight of taxes. A deep, mournful sound, uttered in pain, sorrow or anguish." Turn on the news, observe society, and you will see groaning everywhere, in all nations and countries.

Try to get a clear look at people and nations today, and honestly see the perfect description of today and what the Lord said was coming to planet earth. A "groaning creation" all groans together, including everything God created in the beginning, including beasts, fish, fowls, and humans. All are united in a condition of sorrow. The expression denotes mutual and universal grief. It is one vast and loud lamentation, in which a dying world unites, and in which it has united "until now," today. They are united in sorrow and agony. The common groaning means intense agony, misery, and suffering. No wonder creation looks for deliverance and freedom. Who in their right mind, wants to live in a world of increasing sorrow and agony.

God made a way of escape. That way is His Son, Jesus. Read the verses from Romans again. Christ has interceded for us. He made a way for those who would believe and trust Him. The prophesied end of this place of groaning and travail is in 2 Peter 3:10-13, *"...the day of the Lord will come as a thief in the night; in the which the heavens shall pass away with a great noise, and the elements shall melt with fervent heat, the earth also and the works that are therein shall be burned up. Seeing then that all these things shall be dissolved, what manner of persons ought ye to be in all holy conversation and godliness...Nevertheless we, according to his promise, look for new heavens and a new earth, wherein dwelleth righteousness."* He will make all things new.

Read and study these verses and see that Paul is saying, it's terrible, it's going to get worse, but we are not home yet. Paul gave us these encouraging words, *"Finally, my brethren, be strong in the Lord, and in the power of his might"* (Ephesians 6:10). Christians, it will be worth all earth's suffering and agony. This will be our reward and joy, Revelation 22:3-5, *"...there shall be no more curse: but the throne of God and of the Lamb shall be in it; and his servants shall serve him, And they shall see his face; and his name shall be in their foreheads. And there shall be no night there; and they need no candle, neither light of the sun; for the Lord God giveth them light: and they shall reign forever and ever."* Revelation 22:13, *"...I am Alpha and Omega, the beginning and the end, the first and the last."* Finally, from Isaiah 65:17, His promise has been fulfilled *"For, behold, I create new heavens and a new earth: and the former shall not be remembered, nor come into mind."*

Week #38

THE BITE OF A SNAKE

"He that diggeth a pit shall fall into it; and whoso breaketh an hedge, a serpent shall bite him."
                                                    Ecclesiastes 10:8

I thank God for His immeasurable love for our great nation, the United States of America. He has fulfilled every promise He ever made to these people. He continues to love us and will continue to keep and bless us as long as we follow Him. But, His continued blessing is according to our obedience and overcoming every venomous satanic attack. People who are bitten by snakes are generally not aware the serpent is present. Thus, the bite and the poison are injected with its damage and death when it is too late for help and/or recovery.

Ecclesiastes 10:8 says, *"He that diggeth a pit shall fall into it; and whoso breaketh an hedge, a serpent shall bite him."* What is a hedge? In Scripture it means *"...that which surrounds or encloses..."* As a nation we have always trusted in God for our protection and defense. He has been our hedge. We have believed His promise from Deuteronomy 28:7 *"The Lord shall cause thine enemies that rise up against thee to be smitten before thy face: they shall come out against thee one way, and flee before thee seven ways."* Amen!

The Bible speaks of a *"...space to repent."* In 2 Chronicles 36, God gave the sinful nation of Israel a space to repent after they rejected God, but they did not repent. In the book of Jonah God gave Nineveh a space to repent and they did. These two events reveal the forbearance of the Father. God has graciously granted America, and the world, a space to repent.

Remember Ecclesiastes 10:8 that says, *"He that diggeth a pit shall fall into it; and whoso breaketh an hedge, a serpent shall bite him... (them)."* It's time for Christian believers to fast and pray for our great land. God hears and answers prayer. Pray for Godly conviction that will lead this nation and world to humble repentance. We need to repent for the breaking down of our protective hedge through our indifference to God and going away from His Word and ways. May God have mercy on nations and peoples and save lost souls.

Week #39

SPIRITUAL EROSION

There is a process of things being changed called erosion that is both natural and spiritual. Spiritual erosion can culminate in eternal death. Spiritual erosion is more common than believed because of the way it works. Webster's Dictionary defines erosion as "the process of eroding or being eroded by wind, water, or other natural agents." While natural erosion wears away the earth's surface, spiritual erosion wears away the truth, which then changes Christianity. The exact shape of the earth's surface and the shape of Christianity are altered by erosion.

There are times of flood and wind that change the natural landscape in moments. In his effort to take away convictions and Christian living, some people believe the devil will come and say, "I am the devil, and I've come to kill you spiritually." No, he comes as a thief in the night (1 Thessalonians 5:2), or a wolf in sheep's clothing (Matthew 7:15), or as the father of lies (John 8:44).

The devil does his evil work when he can find his target asleep or unaware that eroding things are slowly taking away and changing even life and death issues. A very serious truth, for another study, is apostasy. The Bible definition for apostasy is "defection", "departure", "revolt" or "rebellion". Many begin this Christian life strong and true. If one is not careful, they begin to question and defect, depart, or even revolt from true convictions and manner of life. The enemy has over 6,000 years of history in attacking a person who is weakened through this defection. It is usually a slow process. Real values and Godly ways begin to change slowly. It's sad but true that the taking away the foundation we were placed on by God through our changing lives is now being taken away.

Have you changed your mind about sin? Is it now easier to overlook and excuse this action against God? Have we developed a compromising spirit with sinners and the world? Do we forsake the assembling of ourselves in true worship and service (Hebrews 10:25)? Time and space prevent the weightier matters of careful study of God's Word and prayer.

These are serious questions. There is a falling away from the Lord *"...for that day shall not come, except there come a falling away first..."* (2 Thessalonians 2:3). We need to examine ourselves (2 Corinthians 13:5). Where there has been an erosion of the things of God, in that self-examination, He will show us the erosion in our lives and call us to return to Him. That revelation will save our souls and make us more than conquerors in Christ Jesus (Romans 8:37).

Week #40

THE ALL-INCLUSIVE WORK OF CALVARY

Jesus, sin and death, eternal punishment, and everlasting life are prevailing subjects of the Bible. But what has escaped most of this generation of the church, outside of preachers that speak of it for profit, is the Divine truth of what Jesus did regarding sickness and healing through His death on the cross. Jesus, the Lamb of God, was slain to fulfill the will of the Father through Him. Having suffered and died at Calvary, He now sits on the throne of victory. He rules, being all-powerful over the world, the flesh, and the devil, not because the Father arbitrarily placed Him there, but through and because of His sufferings.

There is only one way to overcome sin, and that is through the cleansing blood of Jesus. The prophet Isaiah said, *"But he was wounded for our transgressions, he was bruised for our iniquities: the chastisement of our peace was upon him..."* (Isaiah 53:5). That is the forgiveness of sin, but read on in that verse the continuing price that was paid at the same time *"...and with his stripes, we are healed."* Yes, He sits on the throne of sickness and disease. He is the sinner's deliverance from sin, and He is also the physician for the sick.

The miracles of Christ are, at times, called signs and wonders. A sign is defined in the KJV Bible Dictionary as "A wonder; a miracle; a prodigy; a remarkable transaction, event or phenomenon." The dictionary defines wonder as "...the presentation to the sight or mind, of something new, unusual, strange, great, extraordinary, or not well understood; something that arrests the attention by its novelty, grandeur or inexplicableness." There is a manner in which healing for believers, through His redemptive work, is given for His children now, but we also know that there is a time when the trouble of sin and sickness will be forever over in our new bodies.

His sacrificial death demonstrated the love of Jesus. The love of Jesus is equally demonstrated by the gift and promise of Isaiah 53:5, *"...and with his stripes, we are healed."* Unbelievers will argue they know a great Christian who prayed for healing from their sickness and were not healed. There are many Bible examples in answer to this logical question. Space does not permit an in-depth logical explanation, but our accountability before God is to believe His Word and live in His perfect will for our lives. He knows the future and how to guide us through every experience of life.

We need to repent of our sin, and we need to believe His inerrant Word about how He suffered for our health and healing. In your sickness, don't let anything discourage you from trusting God. Study His Word. Lay ahold of His promises. Remember Numbers 23:19 says, *"God is not a man, that he should lie; neither the son of man, that he should repent: hath he said, and shall he not do it? or hath he spoken, and shall he not make it good?"*

Week #41

LOOKING FOR THE 3%

In July of 2020, I preached a message during our annual Missions Convention that I desire to share with you a few brief points from that message.

History reveals that men were considered outstanding in responsibilities, government, war, and hopeless crisis that called upon God for His Divine intervention and control to prevent certain death, ruin, and destruction in times of intense need and darkness. In 1863 during the Civil War, Abraham Lincoln said, "We have forgotten God, too proud to pray that made us. It behooves us then to humble ourselves before the offended power to confess our national sins."

Bible scholars say the word Kairos, an Ancient Greek word, means "a favorable opportunity," and its derivative implies "a right moment, that only lasts a while." In the New Testament, it means "the appointed time in the purpose of God."

It is almost impossible to find governmental leaders and decision-makers who pray or speak of the need for Divine help in our generation. This arrogance, self-reliance, and Godless attitude will lead to certain judgment and total destruction. We need God in every facet of our lives.

I heard some revealing and somewhat surprising statistics about the American Revolutionary War. This war between the American people and the British Empire was for our independence and self-governance. The statistics given were from the First American Revolution fought for our national freedom. I heard it reported that only 3% of the population fought in the war, 10% furnished supplies, 37% fought against us, and 50% did absolutely nothing. I know, shocking and disturbing percentages. That 3% was only a remnant of the total population, but God delivered this new and young nation from their adversary through them.

God had given a spiritual "Kairos" moment. By definition, it will be short-lived, but an opportunity given by God to liberate multitudes that will otherwise be lost for eternity. Please don't miss this opportunity. No matter the odds or tiresome the battle, God says to all in Galatians 6:9, *"And let us not be weary in well doing: for in due season we shall reap, if we faint not."*

On November 22, 1963, before he was assassinated, President Kennedy was on his way to deliver a speech in Dallas, Texas, which contained a brief Scripture. The last paragraph of that undelivered speech to the American people says, "We in this country, in this generation, are - by destiny rather than by choice - the watchmen on the walls of world freedom. We ask, therefore, that we may be worthy of our power and responsibility, that we may exercise our strength with wisdom and restraint, and that we achieve in our time and for all time, the ancient vision of 'Peace on earth, goodwill toward men.' We that must always be our goal, and the righteousness of our cause must always underline our strength. For as was written long ago: *'...Except the Lord keep the city, the watchmen wakeneth but in vain'"* (Psalms 121:7).

Be awakened to this "kairos" opportunity. The Lord is calling. Many lost will be saved. Through this ministry, with your help, vision, and assistance, we are in place to have a great "Christian Revolution" of born-again believers. Contact us today with your commitment to be in that 3%.

Week #42

THAT'S MY KING

For many years I have enjoyed and been blessed by the following text. I will share it with you in the hope you also will be edified and equally blessed as I have been. This minister passed away April 4, 2000, but these words will continue.

That's My King! Do You Know Him?"
by S.M. Lockridge
Pastor of Calvary Baptist Church, San Diego, CA

The Bible says my King is a seven-way king.
He's the King of the Jews; that's a racial king.
He's the King of Israel; that's a national King.
He's the King of Righteousness.
He's the King of the Ages.
He's the King of Heaven.
He's the King of Glory.
He's the King of Kings, and He's the Lord of Lords.
That's my King.
Well, I wonder, do you know Him?
David said, "The Heavens declare the glory of God and the firmament shows His handiwork."
My King is a sovereign King.
No means of measure can define His limitless love.
No far-seeing telescope can bring into visibility the coastline of His shoreless supply.
No barrier can hinder Him from pouring out His blessings.
He's enduringly strong.
He's entirely sincere.
He's eternally steadfast.
He's immortally graceful.
He's imperially powerful.

He's impartially merciful.
Do you know Him?
He's the greatest phenomenon that ever crossed the horizon of this world.
He's God's Son.
He's a sinner's Savior.
He's the centerpiece of civilization.
He stands in the solitude of Himself.
He's awesome.
He's unique.
He's unparalleled.
He's unprecedented.
He's the loftiest idea in literature.
He's the highest personality in philosophy.
He's the supreme problem in higher criticism.
He's the fundamental doctrine of true theology.
He's the cardinal necessity of spiritual religion.
He's the miracle of the age.
He's the superlative of everything good that you choose to call Him.
He's the only one qualified to be an all-sufficient Savior.
I wonder if you know Him today?
He supplies strength for the weak.
He's available for the tempted and the tried.
He sympathizes and He saves.
He strengthens and sustains.
He guards and He guides.
He heals the sick.
He cleanses lepers.
He forgives sinners.
He discharges debtors.
He delivers captives.
He defends the feeble.
He blesses the young.
He serves the unfortunate.
He regards the aged.
He rewards the diligent.

And He beautifies the meek.
I wonder if you know Him?
Well, my King is the King.
He's the key to knowledge.
He's the wellspring of wisdom.
He's the doorway of deliverance.
He's the pathway of peace.
He's the roadway of righteousness.
He's the highway of holiness.
He's the gateway of glory.
Do you know Him? Well!
His office is manifold.
His promise is sure.
His light is matchless.
His goodness is limitless.
His mercy is everlasting.
His love never changes.
His Word is enough.
His grace is sufficient.
His reign is righteous.
And His yoke is easy, and His burden is light.
I wish I could describe Him to you, but He's indescribable.
He's incomprehensible.
He's invincible.
He's irresistible.
You can't get Him out of your mind.
You can't get Him off of your hand.
You can't outlive Him, and you can't live without Him.
The Pharisees couldn't stand Him, but they found out they couldn't stop Him.
Pilate couldn't find any fault in Him. The witnesses couldn't get their testimonies to agree.
Herod couldn't kill Him.
Death couldn't handle Him,
And the grave couldn't hold Him.
Yea! That's my King, Father.

Yours is the Kingdom, and the Power, and the Glory,
Forever and ever, and ever, and ever, and ever.

How long is that?

And when you get through with all the forevers, then, AMEN and AMEN!

(Shadrach Meshach Lockridge (1913-2000) – Pastor of Calvary Baptist Church, San Diego, CA 1953-1993, author, and evangelist.)

Week #43

EVERYONE MUST STRIVE TO ENTER HEAVEN

What more can Jesus do? Is there anything to be added to the work Jesus has already done? Did He fail? Is there more to be done? If so, who is going to do anything that someone might believe needs to be done? NO! It is finished. The Son of God completed the will of the Father. So successful was He in doing the will of the Father that God Himself said of Jesus in Matthew 3:17, *"...This is my beloved Son, in whom I am well pleased."* Revelation 22:18-19 specifies the punishment for those who would add or take away from the perfect work of Jesus Christ. These verses read: *"For I testify unto every man that heareth the words of the prophecy of this book, If any man shall add unto these things, God shall add unto him the plagues that are written in this book: And if any man shall take away from the words of the book of this prophecy, God shall take away his part out of the book of life, and out of the holy city, and from the things which are written in this book."* That is the final and a settled fact.

So, what did Jesus mean in Luke 13:24 when He said, *"Strive to enter in at the strait gate: for many, I say unto you, will seek to enter in, and shall not be able."* If salvation is God's free gift and Jesus has so fully paid the price, why must I strive? Because you have an enemy, the devil, who has come to rob, kill and destroy (John 10:10). The eternal all-sufficient price has been paid, and the enemy comes to take away God's eternal gift. Therefore, we must strive to enter the strait gate. The Bible defines strive as *" to use exertions; to endeavor with earnestness; to labor hard; applicable to exertions of body or mind."* The Bible definition for seek is "To inquire for; to ask for; to solicit; to endeavor to find or gain..."

Jesus is alerting His children that we have a deadly enemy in this life. Jesus included this assurance in 1 John 2:14, *"...I have written unto you, young men, because ye are strong, and the word of God abideth in you, and ye have overcome the wicked one."* We have the devil to overcome in his deadly efforts against us. God has given us this strength and power through faith in Christ. The battle may continue in this life, but we, through Christ, are more than conquerors, found in Romans 8:37.

Continue to fight the good fight of faith (1 Timothy 6:12). Never cease striving, exerting, and laboring hard against Satan. Do not be guilty of just asking and seeking to enter into everlasting life. That is not sufficient to overcome the temptations, lies, and destructive works of hell.

Week #44

A TIME TO ARISE AND SHINE

"Arise, shine; for thy light is come, and the glory of the Lord is risen upon thee. For, behold, the darkness shall cover the earth, and gross darkness the people: but the Lord shall arise upon thee, and his glory shall be seen upon thee. And the Gentiles shall come to thy light, and kings to the brightness of thy rising. Lift up thine eyes round about, and see: all they gather themselves together, they come to thee: thy sons shall come from far, and thy daughters shall be nursed at thy side." Isaiah 60:1-4

These beautiful verses were a promise from the Lord to Israel's children after Israel's 70 years of Babylonian captivity. This same promise is to His church that He said He would have when they would be in trouble. That includes His church today. Remember in God's Word He said in Romans 2:11, *"For there is no respect of persons with God,"* and also in Mark 13:37, Jesus tells us, *"And what I say unto you I say unto all..."* He is always faithful and never fails.

Consider what some of the conditions were in the days of captivity. They suffered through the darkness of a lengthy exile. Their own sin had caused them to be beaten down. God has punished them but never intended to destroy them. He is now going to raise them out of the devastating darkness they have been in. He is the Light they will be in. He seemed to be distant for these years, but now everything is going to change. They must arise and show forth the Light and Glory of their great Deliverer. Verse 2 of Isaiah 60 describes the conditions they were in, *"For, behold, the darkness shall cover the earth, and gross darkness the people: but the Lord shall arise upon thee, and his glory shall be seen upon thee."* Instead of living under the bondage of their enemies, they now are promised in verse 3 and 4 *"...the Gentiles shall come to thy light, and kings to the brightness of thy rising. Lift up thine eyes round about, and see: all they gather themselves together, they come to thee: thy sons shall come from far, and thy daughters shall be nursed at thy side."* Kings will come to their brightness and multitudes will gather to them. (There is much more that needs to be said for even better understanding, but there is a lack of space).

In conclusion, I will use a saint's writings from hundreds of years ago on our day's spiritual truth. He wrote, "As, in the two preceding chapters, the hypocrisy and formality, the profaneness and immorality, that should abound in the latter day, and even among professors of religion, are prophesied of; so, in this, a very ample account is given of latter daylight and glory; of both the spiritual and personal reign of Christ, with the latter of which it concludes. The light and glory of the Church, in the spiritual reign, are described, Isaiah 60:1 the numerous conversions of persons to it from all quarters, east and west particularly, are prophesied of. In Isaiah 60:4, the great usefulness those should be of unto it, in enriching it, and building it up, and in glorifying it, is declared. In Isaiah 60:9, as also the subjection of enemies to it; the favours it should receive from kings, and the fame and renown of it through all nations and ages.

God's people, I believe in the midst of all that we are experiencing in this year of our Lord, TODAY is now the time to arise and shine. In Jesus name, we will.

Week #45

THE SHEPHERD AND THE SHEEP

In my lifetime, I have had little to no experience with sheep. One of my first remembrances was when I was preaching a revival in the state of Tennessee around Christmas time. The church I was ministering in had a float in the annual Christmas parade. Their float consisted of a manger scene in which they were to have live sheep. The people prepared everything in its proper place and only needed to put the live animals on the float. The sheep were nervous and would not step up on the trailer. Someone thought of calling the owner of the sheep. He instructed them to be patient with the animals, and that he would be at the parade site very shortly. When he arrived, we all marveled at what happened. He spoke to the sheep, walked up the ramp, and they followed him without hesitation. The sheep followed the shepherd where he led them.

One of my last pastoral messages was from Luke 15:6-7, where it reads, *"And when he cometh home, he calleth together his friends and neighbours, saying unto them, Rejoice with me; for I have found my sheep which was lost."* He said, *"...I have found my sheep..."* In Psalms 100:3, it is recorded that *"...we are his people, and the sheep of his pasture."*

Why are we likened to sheep when even a casual, general study of sheep is not flattering to the animal because of specific character flaws? For example, sheep have no sense of direction; they are flock animals and will follow other sheep even to a place of death. They are without defense from predators. They are nervous and easily frightened. Yet they are innocent, gentle, and pure.

Another symbol of a lamb is sweetness, forgiveness, and meekness.

Sheep need a shepherd. When a sheep falls, he cannot get up without help. The sheep must be led to clean water and good pasture. A sheep is known to drink muddy water when good water is only feet away. Shepherds put oil on sheep to protect their ears and eyes from parasites. No wonder David said in the 23rd Psalm that the good shepherd (John 10:11) leads into green pastures and beside still waters and restored the soul. Jesus gives the oil of the Spirit to raise a standard against all adversaries and enemies (Isaiah 59:19). Sheep will follow whoever is leading. They have a very poor sense of direction and can be led astray. Sheep are known to have almost no defense mechanism to protect themselves, and when they are wounded, they cannot care for themselves, and in the natural, other animals must lick their wounds.

But there is a strength and invincibility among sheep. Jesus said His people hear His voice and another they would not follow (John 10:27-28 and John 10:5). They may have indecencies, but they make it up with loyalty and awareness. Sheep need a shepherd, and God's people have Jesus who said, *"I am the good shepherd, and know my sheep, and am known of mine"* (John 10:14).

Week #46

TRUTH

We have all heard it said, "the truth hurts." The greatest statement concerning this subject came from Jesus when He said in John 8:32, *"And ye shall know the truth, and the truth shall make you free."* The definition of truth in "Harper's Bible Dictionary" includes the statement that "God is truth." That is the only complete and accurate meaning of the word "truth." One dictionary definition of the word is "actuality or actual existence." Nothing or no one is more real or has "actual existence" but God. Therefore, real truth is a Person. Every personal and human reference to the meaning of truth will someday, like everything of man's flawed concept, fade away, cease to be, and be non-existent.

The Apostle Paul wrote in Romans 3:4, *"...let God be true, but every man a liar..."* When Jesus was being received into heaven from the Mount of Transfiguration, the Father spoke in an audible voice to the disciples saying, *"...This is my beloved Son, in whom I am well pleased; hear ye him"* (Matthew 17:5).

The Words of Jesus are for our learning and admonition. I've often said that sometimes in my life, I had more difficulty knowing what God's will was than I did in obeying the will of God. If an individual knows and loves God, he wants to live his life to please only Him. In prayer one day, I said this to God about the people I preached to in our church congregation; I did not understand why I did not see more obedience from them to live wholly and entirely for Christ. I believe it was the Lord that brought these words to my mind from John 14:15, *"If ye love me, keep my commandments."* In my heart, I knew I must minister to the people on loving God more totally and unselfishly.

When a person loves God as Jesus admonished in Matthew 22:37, *"...Thou shalt love the Lord thy God with all thy heart, and with all thy soul, and with all thy mind,"* that person will not think "the truth hurts," they will be grieved when in any manner they feel they have failed the Lord.

The Word of God says the same thing to every person. When the Lord brings conviction to us, and our hearts and minds are brought to the realization that God has a controversy with us, the things we feel in our emotions and spirits trouble us. The Lord uses these experiences to bring us to the only Savior, Jesus Christ. It is difficult for the moment, but following repentance and confession of sins, a new life begins to bring eternal forgiveness and eternal life. Proverbs 3:11-12 says, *"My son, despise not the chastening of the LORD; neither be weary of his correction: For whom the Lord loveth he correcteth; even as a father the son in whom he delighteth."* Yes, the Lord chastens, but He does so out of love. Come to Christ in true repentance, and you will find mercy and love.

Week #47

THANKS BE TO GOD

This post will be a thanksgiving to God for answered prayer and a testimony to His loving care and protection for one of His children.

February 10th, I received word that an elderly lady I had known for many years and pastored for 26 years was missing, and no one had any thought of where she could be. She is in the beginning stages of Alzheimer's disease. (This is a situation many other people have experienced with a friend or loved one). Her Christian friends and family began to pray for her safety and quick return home. In all honesty, those praying for her had to look beyond the possibilities of what could happen to her and pray in faith that God would intervene. Thankfully, her son-in-law had installed a home camera security system in her home. By that means, they knew exactly what time she left her home and the clothes she was wearing. Thank God for the action of her son-in-law.

She left home without taking her purse, identification, or cell phone. Everyone knew that without God's help, the end of the story could be tragic. Where was she? What had happened to this precious lady? The people of the church and many other believers knew how to touch God. We prayed and asked the Lord to be with her in this crisis.

Thirteen hours later, she was located. God had been with her. In her physical condition, she had driven until she ran out of gas. She was stranded on a remote, two-lane Farm to Market highway, hours from the safety of her home and family, and by now, it was night. She got out of her car and began walking. To where? Someone saw her and called the paramedics to report what they were seeing. The paramedics and police authorities immediately went to help her. They pushed her car into the driveway of a nearby house. Thank God she had been found safe and unharmed. Thank God for the responders that took the situation in hand and professionally assisted her. They searched her car and found contact information placed there by her daughter, and they were able to contact her family.

I have shared this testimony with you as it was told to me. If there is any factual misinformation, it is for that reason. Based on Scripture, I want to give God all of the glory for answered prayer. John 14:13 says, *"And whatsoever ye shall ask in my name, that will I do, that the Father may be glorified in the Son."* In Luke 17:17, Jesus cleansed ten lepers, but only one returned to thank Him, at which time Jesus asked, *"...Were there not ten cleansed? but where are the nine?"*

All glory and praise belong to the One who answered the urgent prayers of those who asked Him!

Week #48

WHO SHALL I SAY SENT ME?

In the third chapter of the Book of Exodus, the miraculous deliverance of God's people from Egyptian bondage is recorded. God is setting His people free from bondage and slavery. He will also fulfill a promise He made to Abraham, Isaac, and Jacob when He said I will free you from the labors of the Egyptians and deliver you from their bondage. I will bring you into the land which I swore to give to Abraham, Isaac, and Jacob, and I will give it to you for a possession. As ancient Egyptian rulers, the pharaohs were both the heads of state and their people's religious leaders. The current pharaoh held them in captivity, but when the Lord sent Moses to bring the people out of their bondage, Moses did not speak to the ruler but to the people who were the captives. In Exodus 3:13, Moses asked God this question, *"...when I come unto the children of Israel, and shall say unto them, The God of your fathers hath sent me unto you; and they shall say to me, What is his name? what shall I say unto them?"* Exodus 3:14 reads, *"And God said unto Moses, I AM THAT I AM: and he said, Thus shalt thou say unto the children of Israel, I AM hath sent me unto you."*

We learn from Exodus 12:40 how long they had been in this Egyptian bondage, *"Now the sojourning of the children of Israel, who dwelt in Egypt, was four hundred and thirty years."* After so many years, it would be natural to ask who sent you to tell us this? The name Moses gave was the correct answer to be given.

The slaves needed encouragement. Moses has been permitted to use the name of the great God who promised that after a long and horrible captivity, He would come and deliver them. His name is the I AM, which means I will become whatever I must become to fulfill My promise. He is assuring them that I AM the sum and total of all existence. There is no one else above Me or before Me. I read where one ancient writer summed it up beautifully by saying, "This signifies the real being of God, His self-existence, and that He is the Being of beings; as also it denotes His eternity and immutability, and His constancy and faithfulness in fulfilling His promises, for it includes all time, past, present, and to come; and the sense is, not only I am what I am at present, but I am what I have been, and I am what I shall be, and shall be what I am."

The most assuring and encouraging thing I can say from the youngest to the oldest Christians is, He is your I AM THAT I AM. The greatest news for the person who has not yet surrendered to His salvation, love, and keeping power is: He wants to be the same "I AM THAT I AM" to you that He has been to all that have surrendered to Him. What a great God He is!

Week #49

MORE VALUABLE THAN GREAT RICHES

Regret! It has often been a sentiment of ourselves, and everyone else, that we have great regrets for actions or words we have committed or said. Statements such as "I would give anything if I could go back and undo..." In these times, taking an acting or speaking a word out of anger or frustration has hurt feelings and ruined friendships. In a worst-case scenario, marriages have been destroyed, and children's lives changed forever. The Bible addresses every facet of life, including such experiences as these events. Proverbs 22:1 tells us, *"A good name is rather to be chosen than great riches..."* That simply refers to our reputation, which we should constantly guard and protect. Why? Your reputation is you, your life. When we have injured our reputation, we think, "I wish I could undo what I did," or "I'm so sorry, I was wrong." But have the destructive seeds we have planted already grown to an irreversible situation? God help us not to justify our behavior, but look to Christ as our example as it is written in 1 Peter 2:21, *"For even hereunto were ye called: because Christ also suffered for us, leaving us an example, that ye should follow his steps."* Peter continued this truth about Christ being an example unto us by saying in 1 Peter 2:23-25 (Only verse 23 quoted), *"Who, when he was reviled, reviled not again; when he suffered, he threatened not; but committed himself to him that judgeth righteously."*

Most people live very self-centered, selfish lives with little or no regard for their reputation or, in the life of a Christian, their testimony. WWJD? What Jesus would do should be considered before a child of God responds or acts in a given situation.

There are some things that are necessary when a person has created a situation that can ruin their reputation or testimony. First, make it right with God, then do everything possible to make it right with the offended person. This is especially true between Christians; Jesus commanded in Matthew 18:15, *"Moreover if thy brother shall trespass against thee, go and tell him his fault between thee and him alone: if he shall hear thee, thou hast gained thy brother."* Churches have been damaged and even possibly been destroyed because of disobedience to this exhortation of the Lord Jesus. Paul wrote Ephesians 4:31-32, *"Let all bitterness, and wrath, and anger, and clamuor, and evil speaking, be put away from you, with all malice: And be ye kind one to another, tenderhearted, forgiving one another, even as God for Christ's sake hath forgiven you."*

I believe it is possible to have a good and Godly reputation restored where there previously was damage. Consider the Apostle Paul and the fear his name (reputation) created in the church and wherever he went. When he met Christ, repented before God, and gave himself to help the very people he previously persecuted, he was valued, loved, and was received as the Man of God that he truly was.

Then, remember the reputation of David following his adulterous affair with Bathsheba. His prayer of repentance in Psalms 51:11, *"Cast me not away from thy presence; and take not thy holy spirit from me."* The forgiveness of God, the restoration He provides is found for David in Psalm 89:26-28, *"He shall cry unto me, Thou art my father, my God, and the rock of my salvation. Also, I will make him my firstborn, higher than the kings of the earth. My mercy will I keep for him for evermore, and my covenant shall stand fast with him."*

Week #50

IN ALL THINGS AND FOR ALL THINGS

"In every thing give thanks: for this is the will of God in Christ Jesus concerning you." 1 Thessalonians 5:18

WOW! In everything, give thanks. When we count and consider the goodness of God to us throughout our lifetime, how can we not be thankful for all of His multiple blessings and workings in our lives. Blessings to forgive, supply needs, and restore our souls. He has done all of this and more many times.

But what about when the experience is threatening, unexplainable, and without understanding? Begin by examining yourself. How may the Lord be working with us now, and for what purpose? He is continually working to make us like Him and finish a more perfect work in us. So, we examine ourselves, and when we know there is no blame in our lives, we submit ourselves to a more perfect work of God in us.

To 1 Thessalonians 5:18, Paul adds Ephesians 5:20 *"Giving thanks always for all things unto God and the Father in the name of our Lord Jesus Christ."* We are to give God all glory in everything and for everything. That is all-inclusive and in and for all things. In fact, it is a command. We look at the momentary matters of life, including our feelings, hurts, desires, and fears which are natural. Still, the ways of God do not always reveal themselves until a later time when it pleases God to reveal His whole purpose in the work He intended from the beginning.

In this scriptural admonition, Believer, fully surrender to obedience and live by faith, and you will see another working of the Holy Spirit in your glorified, eternal life.

Week #51

GOD'S WORD WILL ALWAYS BE PREACHED

There are varying opinions about the continuance of God's Word always being proclaimed on the earth. Some believe it will be in large cathedrals. Others believe that it must be communicated in person to be successfully planted, others think it will be done through the digital domain, etc. I accept all these methods, knowing some will be more successful than others, but I am persuaded any and all means must be employed for the furtherance of God's Word. I can prove that, so please continue reading.

Some think that personality is crucial to communicating God's good and eternal Word. Some preachers use silly humor and others believe props and human inventions must be incorporated. As a minister in this year of our Lord, 2021, I have been privileged to preach in a free land by the traditional and accepted manner of standing on a platform behind a pulpit, endeavoring to minister the truth of the Bible. Only God knows if that method will always be free and available. Whatever comes, His Divine Gospel will always be faithfully and effectively preached.

In a changing world, with changing values involving every facet of life, one of the most serious and damning changes has been toward the Gospel of Christ and everything concerning Christianity. In America and around the world, the institution of Christ-centered preaching and teaching the truth of Christian life are subtlety and openly being subverted. There is open hatred for the things and ways of God. Indeed, throughout human history, Satan has hated and done innumerable measures to stop it. Countless saints and believers have paid, even the supreme price of death, to let the lost and dying know that Jesus died for them, that He loved them, and if they believed in Him, they would be delivered from sin and reign with Him forever. The number who have heard and believed is without number.

Despite evil rulers and God-hating governments that have tried to stamp out the voice of God, it continues now and forever to be sounded. Every devilish effort to prevent the Gospel truth from being declared has failed, and everyone that tries to stop it now and those that will come after us to stop it will also fail. And if they use their anti-God government powers, influence, prestige, and money to subvert the preaching of the infallible Word of God, we know there is a way of God that cannot be killed or stopped by martyrdom, imprisonments, torture, or any other means. When Satan has exhausted every means to prevent God from reaching a lost world with the Gospel, Revelation 14:6 declares, *"And I saw another angel fly in the midst of heaven, having the everlasting gospel to preach unto them that dwell on the earth, and to every nation, and kindred, and tongue, and people."*

Yes, countless multitudes will hear and believe. They will repent of their sin and become children of the Most High God. Revelation 7:9 says, *"After this I beheld, and, lo, a great multitude, which no man could number, of all nations, and kindreds, and people, and tongues, stood before the throne, and before the Lamb, clothed with white robes, and palms in their hands."* God's program can never be stopped!

Week #52

IT WON'T BE LONG
('TIL WE'LL BE LEAVING HERE)

The title of this post is words taken from a gospel song written by Andre Crouch. A few of the words are "count the years as months, count the months as weeks, count the weeks as days, any day now we'll be going home."

There is no way to overstate, nor can any words describe my great joy at this time. Jesus is sure to return very soon. By His grace and love, I'm prepared. Thank God, my immediate family has made themselves ready through the cleansing blood of Jesus. I have only one personal reason to remain here, and that is to share the Gospel of Jesus Christ and cry out for everyone who does not know Him to repent and be saved.

Look at these verses given by the Holy Spirit concerning how swiftly this coming will take. *"In a moment, in the twinkling of an eye, at the last trump: for the trumpet shall sound, and the dead shall be raised incorruptible, and we shall be changed,"* said the Apostle Paul in 1 Corinthians 15:52. Jesus said in Matthew 24:27, *"For as the lightning cometh out of the east, and shineth even unto the west; so shall also the coming of the Son of man be."* This promised return of Christ will be in a moment, in the twinkling of an eye, and as lightning. All preparations for anyone to be ready for His return are to be made now while there is an opportunity to come to Christ and be cleansed from sin.

In Matthew 16, Jesus said some people could read natural signs and miss the most important signs of the spiritual. The people wanted a sign from heaven to which

"He answered and said unto them, When it is evening, ye say, It will be fair weather: for the sky is red. And in the morning, It will be foul weather to day: for the sky is red and lowering. O ye hypocrites, ye can discern the face of the sky; but can ye not discern the signs of the times?" (Matthew 16:2-3)

Signs relative to the coming of the Lord Jesus are growing exponentially every day. Read the Bible, pray for enlightenment, and take a look at the evidence that "it won't be long 'til we'll be leaving here." Look at the signs created by sin. Look at the signs generated by government and politics. New peace accords are being heralded and bringing false hope for world peace. This attempt at peace is spoken of in Scripture as an act that will bring "sudden destruction." 1 Thessalonians 5:3 is where you read this proclamation *"For when they shall say, Peace and safety; then sudden destruction cometh upon them, as travail upon a woman with child; and they shall not escape."*

For the Christian believer, these are great and momentous times. It is saying to us that our labors are almost completed. We know that we will soon see our precious Lord and remain with Him eternally.

Let me urge and encourage you to make sure you are personally a Child of Christ. Repent and ask for His mercy and great Salvation. He will accept and receive you unto Himself.

We wish to acknowledge the writing and authors that portions of this book are taken from. If somehow, we have inadvertently included a work with a copyright still in force, please let us know and we will make immediate changes. If any copyright infringement has occurred, it was unintentional. All Scripture quotations are taken from the King James Version of the Bible unless otherwise specified.

Made in the USA
Columbia, SC
10 August 2024